**Suffolk Cou**

A

CW00687081

Libraries &

'The
doct
whic

'This
polit
thou
sumi
trans
out.
phil
scho

Jean
the r
an e
Fren
Univ
at th

Janet
Class
Fren
Jacqu
Naqu

Chris
Exete
Atlar

30127 06113589 8

Plato and the City

A New Introduction to Plato's Political Thought

Jean-François Pradeau

translated by Janet Lloyd

with a Foreword by Christopher Gill

UNIVERSITY
of
EXETER
PRESS

First published in 1997 in French as
Platon et la cité by Presses Universitaires de France

This translation published in 2002 by
University of Exeter Press
Reed Hall, Streatham Drive
Exeter, Devon EX4 4QR
UK
www.ex.ac.uk/uep/

British Library Cataloguing in Publication Data
A catalogue record for this book is available from
the British Library

Hardback ISBN 0 85989 653 6
Paperback ISBN 0 85989 654 4

Typeset in 10/12pt Sabon by
Kestrel Data, Exeter, Devon

Printed in Great Britain by
Antony Rowe Ltd, Chippenham, Wiltshire

to Luc Brisson and Christopher Gill

Contents

Translator's Note		ix
Foreword by Christopher Gill		xi
Author's Note		xvii
Introduction		1
1	'I am no politician' (Socrates)	9
	Socrates against his city	9
	The wrecking of the Athenian maritime empire:	
	the *Menexenus*	14
	Political competence	36
2	The political psychology of the *Republic*	43
	The great soul that is the city	43
	Serving the city	53
	Political science (and politics)	65
3	Producing the city: the *Statesman*	72
	The conditions necessary for political technique	72
	The object of politics	81
	Political demiurgy	90
	Laws and ways of life	99
4	The life of the city: the *Timaeus-Critias*	114
	The world of the city	114
	The political living being	119

5 The city, a world of politics: the *Laws* 133
  The laws of the constitution 135
  The constitution of the city 139
  The order of the world 156

Conclusion 167
Bibliography 169
Index 177

Translator's Note

I have used the following translations of ancient texts:

Plato, *Complete Works*, edited with an introduction and notes by
    J.M. Cooper, Indianapolis/Cambridge, Hackett, 1997.
Critias (translated by Diskin Clay), *Laws* (translated by T.J.
    Saunders, first edition 1970), *Statesman* (C.J. Rowe, first
    edition, 1995).

For all other Plato texts, the Loeb Classical Library, Cambridge,
Mass./London, Harvard University Press.

Apology, Crito, in Volume 1, translated by Harold North Fowler,
    1966 (first edition 1914).
Cratylus, Parmenides in Volume 4, translated by Harold North
    Fowler, 1966 (first edition 1926).
Euthydemus, Laches, in Volume 2, translated by W.R.M. Lamb,
    1990 (first edition 1924).
Gorgias, in Volume 3, translated by W.R.M. Lamb, 1925.
Menexenus, Timaeus, in Volume 9, translated by R.G. Bury, 1981
    (first edition 1929).
Republic in Volume 5 (Books 1–5) and 6 (Books 6–10), translated
    by Paul Shorey, 1956 (Vol. 5, first edition 1930, Vol. 6, first
    edition 1935).

Also in the Loeb Classical Library:
Thucydides, *The History of the Peloponnesian War*, translated by
    Charles Forster Smith, 1991 (first edition 1923).

Foreword
by Christopher Gill

This book is a translation of a revised and extended version of Jean François Pradeau's *Platon et la cité*, first published in France in 1997.[1] What does the book have to offer English-speaking readers?

In the first instance, as the title indicates, this is both a study of a specific theme in Plato—the 'city' or political community—and an introduction to Plato's political thought as a whole. It is lucid and non-technical; it includes summaries of the main dialogues relevant to this theme and translations of key extracts; all Greek terms are translated throughout. It thus provides an accessible survey of a major topic in Greek philosophy and political theory for a wide range of students, scholars and general readers.

But this book also has an original and distinctive approach to its subject. Jean-François Pradeau, who teaches at the University of Paris-X Nanterre, is widely recognized by specialists as one of the most gifted and original of younger Plato scholars. He is the author of a major study of the Atlantis story as well as of editions (translations with introductions and notes) of four Platonic dialogues. This book offers a valuable point of access to the unified and systematic

1. Paris, Presses universitaires de France, 1997.

reading of Plato that is characteristic of much contemporary French scholarship.

It may be helpful to spell out more fully how Pradeau's approach differs from the characteristic standpoint of much Plato scholarship in English. Since the Second World War, there have been two overriding preoccupations in English-language Plato scholarship. One is the question of Plato's attitude to democracy. The other is the question of how Plato's thought developed, especially in his later works, after the *Republic*.

Karl Popper, reacting against the rise of Fascism and of totalitarianism in the inter-war years, famously described Plato as an 'enemy of the Open Society'. The debate about whether Plato was or was not an opponent of democracy had a pervasive influence on much post-war scholarship on Plato, particularly on the *Republic*.[2] A reaction of a different kind to the rise of Fascism in the 1930s underlies the work of Leo Strauss, a German emigré whose writings have had a huge, though controversial, influence, especially in the USA. Strauss maintained that Plato's message in the *Republic* was that philosophers could have no effective influence on political life and should concern themselves purely with the search for truth. This message (Strauss claimed) is conveyed in an oblique, self-concealing style that only skilfully trained academic readers can decode. Right-wing American in-tellectuals have taken the Straussian reading of Plato as support for their rejection of political programmes of social improvement in the USA.[3]

A second preoccupation of English-language Plato scholar-ship in the last fifty years has been with a supposed development in Plato's later thought. The *Republic* has been seen as the classic text of Platonic Utopian idealism. The political structure outlined there (centred on the idea of

2. Popper, 1945; Bambrough, 1967. For a new treatment of this theme, see Samaras, 2002.
3. Strauss, 1964; for discussions see Burnyeat, 1985, and Ferrari, 1997.

philosophers as rulers) has been taken as a constitutional blueprint that Plato would like to see realized in real life. In his later works, the *Statesman, Timaeus-Critias* and the *Laws*, Plato is thought to have become gradually convinced that this blueprint could never be realized. He turned towards a more constitutional model (the law-bound state), though he adopted this only as a 'second-best' to the ideal state of the *Republic*.

Pradeau's book forms a welcome contrast to both these scholarly tendencies. A key theme in his book, which has a bearing on both tendencies, is that Plato's political philosophy is not primarily centred on *constitutional* thought (including thought about democracy) at all. What Plato is trying to define are certain core ideas, which apply to political life in all types of constitution, and which are significant for non-political life as well. The chief of these is the idea that politics is—or should be—an art or craft, a form of knowledge, grounded in objective principles. A central role of this art is that of creating a community that is genuinely unified; and, without this art, no community can achieve real unity.

As Pradeau brings out, this means that Plato is neither anti- nor pro-democratic, any more than he is (as he has often been thought to be) pro-Spartan, pro-aristocratic or pro-monarchical. This is not to deny that Plato's dialogues imply certain views or responses to Athenian democracy. Pradeau shows, revealingly, how Plato's *Menexenus*, a pastiche funeral oration to Athenians who have died in war, gives a picture of Athens' deterioration in the fifth century, which implies a critique of Athenian democratic political culture. Also, in the Laws, Plato imagines a form of politico-economic life in which the Athenian democratic ideal of equality was realized, though in a radically different constitutional pattern. But, in both cases, Plato's response to (Athenian-style) democracy is dictated by his larger conceptual approach, which is not fundamentally linked with constitutional forms at all.

Pradeau's book also forms a marked contrast to most developmental readings of Plato's thought. He sees a single line of thought, centred on the role of knowledge as an art which unifies the city, running throughout Plato's works, from the early, supposedly 'Socratic', dialogues to the *Laws*, Plato's last work. The variations between the dialogues do not indicate change in these core ideas. Rather, different dialogues have different conceptual projects which examine various aspects of these ideas. Pradeau shows how, in a series of dialogues, including the *Euthydemus* as well as the *Republic*, Plato works out the idea of knowledge of the good as both a determinate kind of expertise and one that can guide the management of other functions. In the *Republic*, the central theme for exploration is that such knowledge can operate both at the psychological and socio-political level and that this is the only force that can bring real unity to the functions of both personality and state. Without the direction of such knowledge, all political constitutions and psychological conditions are more or less incoherent.

Although the *Republic* is widely thought of as Plato's central political work, in fact it explicitly cuts across the boundaries of the psychological and the political, and does not, as Pradeau underlines, define a specifically *political* art at all. It is the *Statesman* that focuses on the distinctive form of political art, characterized by the combination of objective knowledge of the good and the ability to unify the different elements in the community by a process of 'weaving' through education. It is also the *Statesman* that explores such centrally political questions as the relationship between government and law and between government through executive action and through con-stitutional forms.

The *Statesman* is sometimes seen as marking the start of a process in which Plato renounces the hope of realizing the ideal that philosophers could become rulers and settles for a 'second-best', government by constitutional laws.

Pradeau argues that this is not how we should understand the thought of Plato's later dialogues. Plato retains his conviction that knowledge of the good should govern the direction of politics; but in the dialogues after the *Republic*, he explores the idea that such knowledge can be embodied in constitutional structures and codes of laws as well as direct executive government. Rather than seeing these later dialogues as marking a philosophical retreat, Pradeau sees them as conceptually adventurous, as Plato presses in different directions the idea of knowledge-based political frameworks.

In the *Timaeus-Critias*, Plato links the study of political expertise and order with that of the physical universe. The Atlantis story serves as a vehicle for exploring the physical aspects of political life and for depicting the contrast between the rationally based, unified state and its opposite in terms of the use of land and of material culture. In the *Laws*, his last and longest work, Plato works out in the fullest and most systematic way the thought that political art or knowledge could pervade and unify the life of an entire community. Political art in this case is seen as expressed by a combination of direct government, constitutional forms, laws accompanied by public explanation, education and custom, and is conceived as operative in the entire material, social and cultural life of a community.

The *Laws* has often been seen as Plato's dullest and least philosophically coherent work. Pradeau presents it as Plato's political masterpiece, the culmination of his vision of a community unified by political art.

Although Pradeau's book marks a contrast with much earlier English-language scholarship, his ideas have parallels in some recent scholarship. Certain British and American scholars are also questioning the standard picture of development in Plato's political philosophy and in Plato's thought more generally.[4] This gives an added interest to Pradeau's compelling statement of the unified reading of

Plato's political thought. His book is both a striking and suggestive academic study in its own right and a valuable introduction to a perennially fascinating aspect of Plato's philosophy.

4. Scepticism about the standard picture of Plato's chronology and of development in English-language scholarship is expressed by, for instance, Cooper, 1997, pp. xii–xvii; Kahn, 1996, ch. 2. The standard picture of Platonic political development has been questioned especially by Rowe, 2000, pp. 233–57, esp. 244–51. See, more generally, Annas and Rowe, forthcoming.

Author's Note

The aim of my study is to show the basis of the coherence of
Plato's political doctrine, but also to provide an introduction
to the principal texts in which this doctrine is explained. For
that reason, each chapter contains a more or less detailed
account of the structure of the dialogues mentioned.

Introduction

It is impossible to conceive of many without one
Parmenides, 166b1–2.

At the time of Plato's birth in 428 BC, Athens had been at war with the Spartans and their allies for the past three years, and was still reckoning the number of those who had died in the terrible plague epidemic that had carried off over a quarter of her population in 430–429. In the year of his death, 347, when the Athenian empire was no more than a distant memory, King Philip of Macedon was officially admitted to the group of Greek powers of which he would soon be the master. Plato was not concerned to describe and analyse that twilight of Athenian democracy; rather, he tried to hasten it. But to that end he adopted neither of the two paths open to an educated Athenian gentleman hostile to democracy, namely either that of conservative ideological commitment or that of scholarly constitutional criticism. Instead, he chose the path of philosophy and political thought.

The noble origin of the philosopher, who came from one of the most powerful Athenian families, reserved him a special place in the group of aristocrats hostile to democracy. He rejected this, just as he appears always to have refused to defend any of the interest groups in his city. Nor did Plato engage in an examination of the conditions in which power

[1]

was exercised or of the functioning of the city's institutions, with a view to reforming them or seeking an alternative to them. Such work, involving enquiry and observation, was probably carried out in the school that Plato had opened in Athens in about 387, the Academy, the purpose of which was in part political, as it trained its students to take part in city affairs.[1] The Platonic dialogues eschew examination of the different kinds of existing political constitutions with a view to reforming or diluting them (a type of examination that we do find in the works of Aristotle, one of Plato's pupils). Rather than criticize the governments or institutions of past or present cities for their defects or their in-adequacies, and rather than denounce particular kinds of civil laws or particular forms of public deliberation, the philosopher evolved an unprecedented critique, the aim of which was to replace all known forms of political organi-zation by theoretical perfection stemming from thought about the city.

The Platonic hypothesis upon which this 'political philosophy' is founded[2] is that theoretical research is relevant to politics: politics needs speculation, the subject of which is not the present situation or a history of political powers, but rather the nature of life lived in common, the way to live a communal life. Politics that is not based on such research and analysis will be vain indeed. If one does not know what communal life is, if one understands nothing of its origins, its conditions and its objectives, city life simply means a life of conflict and power struggles; and politics is

1. Baltes, in an essential study, assembles and examines all the information that we possess on the Platonic Academy: Baltes, 1993, pp. 5–26.
2. The expression 'political philosophy' perhaps calls for inverted commas, as the idea of a 'political' genre of philosophy does not fit at all well with the way in which Plato associates philosophical thought and political thought. Badiou, a contemporary and acute Platonist, judiciously under-lines the ambiguities implicit in a 'political philosophy'; see in particular Badiou, 1992.

[2]

just a name for the means that serve this, just a technique of domination. When the dialogues speak of Athens and the Greek world, that is what they are attacking. On the basis of the project of defining the nature of the city and what is best for it, Plato's philosophical critique calls into question the very existence of cities, whether Greek or otherwise. It calls into question the very basis of Plato's co-citizens' belief that they all belong to the same community, a single city united by the bonds of law and language. Plato claims that the Athenian democracy is no more a city than its neighbours with oligarchic or monarchic regimes, and that all these regimes are merely gatherings which, although they may in some cases be founded upon good customs and reasonable laws, nevertheless remain *corrupt* gatherings, incapable of bringing about what is, after all, their common goal: a communal life. Not a good, happy, or fine communal life, simply a mode of life shared in common by all the citizens, who are linked together within the unity of one and the same city.

Corruption, which precisely defines the process of the destruction of a living being, is the state in which Plato's contemporaries find themselves. Briefly, he notes that men do not live well in 'cities' that have bad constitutions and are badly governed. What is wrong is not the outcome of a historical process, as is claimed by the reactionary partisans of oligarchy, who lay the blame on the moral decadence of Athens ever since the Persian Wars at the beginning of the fifth century. The real threat to all gatherings of human beings are conflicts and dissensions; alarming examples of these are provided by the Athenian democracy, which meanwhile continues to repeat the same old lie: namely, that all its citizens are capable of everything and that each one has a hand in governing the city. Democratic propaganda (which, as Plato clearly shows, serves only a handful of masters) and its sophistic variant can produce and diffuse only simulacra that bestow upon the factions, the citizens' conflicts, and the prevailing confusion of opinions no more than the appearance of a city, a real state, and the search for the truth. The Platonic political critique, in contrast, sets out to show that a gathering of human beings does not necessarily constitute a single city, that conflict is not a normal mode of communal life and that an opinion is not the same as the knowledge of truth. Such a critique, of course, demands that the city be first defined, along with the conditions for its unity and a mode of communal life that might possibly avoid conflict and corruption; and it also requires that knowledge of the truth be defined. That is precisely the programme adopted by the *Republic*, for that dialogue associates the quest for the truth with a quest for political perfection. But it is also the programme adopted by the *Statesman*, the *Critias* and the *Laws*, to which the main part of this study will be devoted. The present work aims above all to underline the innovative nature of Plato's observations and political priorities, and then to show how well and with what determined coherence he formulated these.

All the Platonic dialogues remain faithful to the hypothesis according to which *politics stems from thought* From that hypothesis, it is possible to reconstitute and understand the four principal features of Plato's political doctrine.

1. A situation or context: the critique of Athenian democracy as a corrupting condition for the human individual (in Athens he is an unhappy citizen, a living being who is sick and either the possessor of inadequate knowledge or just plain ignorant). This situation prompts:

2. the decision to subordinate the constitution of the human group to what is the best thing in human beings, namely, knowledge (an understanding mind). Plato therefore decides to make the government of the city dependent upon knowledge of the truth. That decision is supported by:

3. the Greek conviction that the destiny of knowledge and

[4]

that of communal life are linked, that there can be no thought without some form of political organization, nor can there be any good politics without genuine thought. That hypothesis, that decision, and that conviction then lead to:

4. a conclusion as to the nature of the city and the meaning of the very term 'politics'. As we shall see, this is not a term much favoured by the dialogues. They are deliberately vague about this activity, referring to it sometimes as a 'royal technique', sometimes as a 'political technique', sometimes as 'political science'; sometimes again they describe it as active, sometimes as productive, sometimes as theoretical. The reader can never get anywhere by enquiring into the status of politics in Plato. That politics exists is true: there is a political technique or science which, like any technique, is a kind of knowledge. But all that should really matter are the object and nature of that knowledge. The object of politics is the unity of the city; and the knowledge that is suited to that object is philosophy.

The unified city, the elaboration of which is the purpose of these Platonic dialogues, only really exists in those dialogues: it is a mode of reflection, of thought, and of discourse too (*logos*). Plato wants to entrust the foundation and government of the city solely to thought. Already in his earliest texts he declares that the government of the city cannot result naturally from a kind of animal grouping, nor can it result from, or express, an opinion, even a majority opinion, nor be confused with any particular skill (governmental know-how). Attacking Athens, Plato says that the city is not a market, nor an army, nor a court of law: so a governor cannot behave as a merchant (satisfying certain interests), nor as a military commander (incapable of educating those whom he leads), let alone as a lawyer (flattering clients and lying). A governor can only behave in accordance with thought, with the reflection indispensable for the conception of a city: he must be a philosopher, for that is the name given to a man who is able to devote the best part of himself (his soul) to thought concerning communal life, a man whose thinking strives for the true unity of the city. The Platonic dialogues always allot the philosopher that same function (the very exercise of which makes him a philosopher): namely, as one who possesses knowledge, to assume the function of government. That function needs to be exercised in order to give life to the city, that is to say, in particular, to get citizens to live together and arrange for their modes of life, skills and activities to harmonize in unity and mutual tolerance. So what needs to be elucidated is the nature of the city and the manner in which philosophy must understand it in order to render possible the political institution of a new mode of life.

Concentrating on the city enables one to understand the particular way in which Plato intervenes in the domain of political thought and to collect together and then set out the principal themes of his political theory. (These are his presentation of the best or most desirable political regime, of his 'classes' of citizens, their modes of life, their techniques and skills, the nature and exercise of power, and the status of institutions and laws.) One then comes to see how, gradually, the city becomes the principal subject of that theory and of its most remarkable variations. It is, no doubt, because Plato's œuvre as a whole manifests a sustained thematic coherence, unaffected by the dramatic upheavals that some scholars seek to detect, that the variations and the introduction of new methods of research and new subjects from one group of dialogues to another are all the more significant. Just as the decisive question of the 'intelligible forms' is already raised in the earliest dialogues, although these only deal with it in an unresolved, tentative or incomplete manner compared with the more conclusive treatment of the *Phaedo*, the *Parmenides*, and the *Timaeus*, so too the question of the city, in its turn, can be seen to be

[6]

the subject of a growing preoccupation in Plato's oeuvre as a whole.[3]

The intention of the present work is to show that Plato's political critique, as briefly described above, is not elaborated as a political doctrine until the point at which it takes the city as a subject suited to the critical enquiries characteristic of what we call the 'early dialogues'.[4] It is Plato who makes the city the point at which philosophical speculation, polemics against the sophists and the ideologues of democracy, and the critique launched against existing constitutions all converge. What is at stake is, clearly, always the same: Plato enters the Athenian debate with the purpose of setting up the project of a government of knowledge in opposition to the corruption of contemporary mores and

3. I should like to express my gratitude to British scholarship and take this opportunity to say that my interpretation of Plato places me fairly and squarely on the side of those who support a 'unitarian' interpretation of Plato's œuvre and that this leads me to reject the hypothesis that it suffered from chronological upsets and breaks in the course of its 'development'. The plan of my present study therefore follows the most generally accepted chronology for the Platonic dialogues purely for reasons of convenience (for details, see n. 4 below). As will be seen, this chronological arrangement in no way undermines the coherence of Plato's political doctrine.

4. All the chronological hypotheses should be treated with caution, but in general historians of Platonism agree in dating the production of the dialogues to four periods. According to this theory, Plato (428–347 BC) first, between 399 and 390, wrote those which are known as the 'early' dialogues, the *Hippias 1* and *Hippias 2*, the *Alcibiades* (if, as in my case, its authenticity is acknowledged: see my introduction to Pradeau, 2002), the *Ion*, the *Laches*, the *Charmides*, the *Euthyphro*, the *Protagoras* and the *Lysis*; between 390 and 385, the *Apology*, the *Crito*, the *Cratylus*, the *Menexenus*, the *Meno*, the *Euthydemus* and the *Gorgias*; between 385 and 370, roughly, the *Republic*, the *Phaedo*, the *Phaedrus* and the *Symposium*; and between 370 and Plato's death, finally, the *Theatetus*, the *Parmenides*, the *Sophist*, the *Statesman*, the *Philebus*, the *Timaeus*, the *Critias* (unfinished) and the *Laws*, on which Plato may have been working at the time of his death.

Some recent studies call into question some familiar assumptions about Platonic chronology: see e.g. Kahn, 1996, ch. 2 and Cooper, 1997.

minds, denouncing democracy's essential inability to encourage the necessary transformation of the existing modes of life, and defining the city as the mixed living reality in which it is possible for human beings to attain to the perfection of which they are capable. His city thus stems simultaneously from speculative enquiry (we must discover its nature), a historical and ideological critique (we must protect it from the kinds of corruption, past and present, to which it is vulnerable), and a normative programme of research (we must construct it, arrange it and govern it in accordance with certain norms and certain ends). In this book, we shall try to follow those various strands, keeping to the order in which the dialogues are presumed to have been written, and emphasizing the fact that at first Plato only focused on the city by way of a comparison (or an analogy) or comparative digression. Up until the *Statesman*, his political doctrine is mediated in this way, elaborating a dual discourse in which the terms serve to define both the city and whatever it is being compared to. The *Republic* refers both to the individual *and* the city: political discourse is also a 'psychology'. The *Statesman* refers both to 'tissue' *and* the city: here political discourse becomes a 'technology'. Thereafter, Plato's doctrine merges the unity of the city, which is its primary and constant concern, with the life of the city, and political discourse, now linked with cosmology, becomes a 'zoology' or 'politogony'.

1

'I am no politician' (Socrates)

Socrates against his city

Plato's earliest dialogues, the ones described as 'Socratic', tackle the political question hardly at all and do not make the city the subject of any specific enquiry. It is not possible to explain this silence simply by reference to the somewhat ambiguous and ultimately very anecdotal declarations that the principal figure in these dialogues, namely Socrates, makes regarding his own political commitment. The man who said at his trial, 'You may be sure, men of Athens, that if I had undertaken to go into politics, I should have been put to death long ago' (*Apology* 31d7–9)[5], also claims in the *Republic* that his *daimon* (or rather, his 'divine sign') prevents him from taking part in the affairs of the city. But this is a way of begging the question that Plato's favourite character is forever repeating, stating in the same conversation that he is not a politican and, at the same time, that he knows more about the subject than anybody else.[6]

---

5. See also the *Gorgias*, from which the title of this first chapter is borrowed ('I am no politician', at 473e7).
6. On the figure and character of Socrates, depending on whether one is interested in the 'historical' Athenian philosopher or his presence in the texts of Plato, Xenophon and Aristotle, see Vlastos, 1991; Vlastos, 1994. See also Penner, 1992, pp. 121–69, and 'Socrates', in Rowe, 2000, pp. 164–89.

Socrates the Athenian, who on three occasions defended his city with exemplary courage, does not vote (claiming he is incapable of doing so), nor does he attend the Assembly (the *Ecclesia*), or the courts of law. But, although he steers clear of the affairs of the democratic city and all elective, deliberative, and judiciary procedures, it is the better to denounce them within the Athenian Walls, beyond which he seldom ventures and then only because of the war or in order to listen to some talk that interests him.[7] The abstension from the functions of citizenship thus correlates directly with the pedagogy and polemics engaged in by the philosopher who, although he does not vote, declares that he is useful to his city, devoted to the fight for justice (*Apology* 31e–32a) and finally, 'one of the few, not to say the only one in Athens who attempts the true art of statesmanship, and the only man of the present time who puts that art into practice' (*Gorgias* 521d6–8). The declarations of the character Socrates may be peremptory, but they are by no means contradictory. What he draws attention to are the point of view and the competence of one single citizen, unique in his political behaviour. Socrates, as a critical individual, adopts a position that may be described as 'generic', if not 'dogmatic'. It is in the name of knowledge and norms alien to the kind of political affairs organized and directed by the Athenian democracy that Socrates abstains from performing his functions as a citizen, but it is on the grounds of that knowledge and his understanding of those norms that he allows himself to criticize his city. His critique is generic, not specific, in the sense that it attacks the government and the life of the city in the name of the norms of what is good, true and just, without ever specifying how a 'good' assembly or a 'just' magistracy would function, or what a 'true' constitution might be. As can be seen—and this is the reason

7. As in *Phaedrus*, 230b–e. The expression 'city affairs' or, as is more common, 'political affairs', translates the Greek *politika pragmata*, 'political things'.

why Socratic pronouncements are always so ambiguous in those early dialogues—the elements and criteria of his philosophical critique of Athenian democracy remain distant from the reality of government in the city.

In both the *Apology* and the later *Gorgias*, Socrates always seems concerned about the fate of his city and his co-citizens: he points out the contradictions and failings of both in similar terms, always criticizing the absence of the conditions necessary for the realization of the norms indispensable for their excellence. What the Athenians are suffering from is a deficiency of virtue. The corrupt city that is sinking ever further into demagogy and violence is thus exposed to injustice, impiety, ignorance and malice. In opposition to it, Socrates sets its contrary and remedy, in the form of a list of virtues (excellences), a catalogue of which is the substance of the early dialogues.[8] At a superficial reading, one might assume the Socratic critique to be a *moral* critique of political corruption, but that is not the case. Not only does Plato make no distinction, as Aristotle was to, between ethics and politics (both are ruled by the same norms, and an individual has no private, autonomous existence distinct from his existence as a citizen), but furthermore, and above all, Socrates' critique always remains a political critique. What it accuses or deplores are the institutions, the way in which power is exercised, the behaviour of groups of citizens and the imperiousness of the city's leaders. But it never suggests any alternative, never envisages any specific form of political organization that might be opposed to or take the place of the corrupt city. It no more occurs to Socrates to pass judgement on the Athenian democracy by reference to the edge that the constitutions of other cities might possibly have over it than, as yet, to construct a plan or theoretical model of a city that is excellent. He never condemns Athenian democracy on the grounds that the oligarchic regime of Sparta is superior to it.

8. On this subject, see Brisson, 1993, pp. 75–92.

Contrary to what Callicles suggests,[9] Socrates is never wholly in favour of the arguments of the pro-Sparta party. Thus the city never becomes the true object of philosophical reflection. These dialogues never grant it the status of a specific subject of research.

One correlative of, but not reason for, this omission from the theoretical research project of the dialogues is the allegorical embodiment of the city. When Socrates condemns Athens, he always refers to it as though to a person who deserves reproof because of his moral deficiency or competence or who has, regrettably, been led astray. In the early dialogues, the city is thus presented in a personified form which makes it possible for Socrates to appeal to it as to a father or mother (most notably in the *Apology* 24b9 and 26b5 and in the *Crito*, in which we find the formula, 'the city, your country [or father]' (*hê polis kai hê patris*, 51b9–c1)[10], and to denounce those who do not offer it the homage and devotion that are its due. This allegorical aspect of Athenian patriotism is not peculiar to Plato. It is also to be found in the tragic poets, the orators and the ideologues, regardless of whether or not they favour democracy. However, it is given an unusual twist in Plato's critical perspective, in which the person of Athens is represented as either sick or badly served. The position that he adopts in this way in political debate thus stands out as exceptional. What he attacks is, precisely, what has seemed to create unanimity—so much so, indeed, that even groups of

9. In the *Gorgias*, 515e, where Callicles criticizes Socrates for frequenting the 'men with torn ears' (the Athenian partisans of Sparta engaged in violent wrestling which mutilated their ears). However, no pro-Spartan propaganda is to be found in the dialogues, nor does Plato ever give his total approval to any foreign constitutions as a possible alternative to democracy.

10. The most extreme example of this personification is that of the laws of Athens who become Socrates' interlocutor in *Crito*, 50a–54c. But such personifications are also common in the rest of the Platonic corpus, e.g. the end of the *Alcibiades* 133d–134e.

Athenian society with different interests have all seemed to find ground for agreement on this point: namely, the supremacy of Athens and its natural hegemony over the rest of the Greek world. The partisans of oligarchy and the defenders of democracy were all in agreement (their consensus really only dissolved between 380 and 370) on the defence of Athens' necessary imperialism, which was rather vaguely justified by the alleged excellence of the city and its citizens. Plato shatters the enchantment of this ideological consensus by making three assertions.

1. Irreducible conflicts exist in the city, the most visible being the clash of interests between the two most firmly established parties,[11] and the existence of such groups (even more than the possibility that one or the other may take over the government of the city) is a sign of an irremediable state of dissension (*stasis*).
2. Heroic Athens, the favoured city chosen by the gods, is not the city that now exists: perfection, which might indeed justify political hegemony, is not an attribute of contemporary Athens.
3. Opposing the notion that the Athenians *are* Athens and that the former and the latter are equally glorious, Plato declares that the Athenians of his day are treating Athens wrongly: they are harming it and fall far short of the stature of the heroes of the past. The Platonic critique is unsettling because, right from the start, it is levelled against the common political myth, the basis of which is based on the idea of the extended existence of a powerful city called Athens, whose citizens are altogether

11. The party of 'the few', the 'oligarchic' party, that is, the party of the well-born; and the 'democratic' party of the people, or the majority. It is important both to be wary of this opposition, as it does not coincide exactly with the relations of the forces of Athenian political life, but also to retain it, as the Athenians themselves used it to summarize their political conflicts. Plato repeatedly declares that this opposition was the very symptom of the corruption of the city (split in two by the conflict between its parties).

exceptional. That idea, says Plato, is not just a fiction, but a positive lie.

The wrecking of the Athenian maritime empire: the *Menexenus*

In the month of October in every year of warfare—probably ever since the Persian Wars—Athens paid public homage to its soldiers who had died in battle. On this occasion of civic funeral rites, a funeral oration was pronounced, in the presence of the soldiers' remains. The funeral oration was a genre with well-defined constraints and motifs. It was expected to praise the courage of the dead and to exhort and console those who survived them. Such an oration, in three parts (praise, exhortation, consolation) was more than simply a funeral ceremony. It was an opportunity for the city, gathered together before those who had died for it, to consecrate its own work. As Nicole Loraux has shown, the funeral oration was political discourse, one of the types of discourse particularly favoured by the Athenian democracy. It used this discourse to represent itself as being, right from the start, completely different from other cities, pledged to defend all the Greeks through the free exercise of its bravery, and all the more powerful because it was composed of an exceptional people, totally united both by birth and by law.[12] As he praised the dead, the orator at the same time thus saluted the living, for they were all united in that they shared the same citizenship. In this respect he followed many other orators, such as Gorgias and Thucydides (who reported the funeral speech delivered by Pericles at the end of the first year of the Peloponnesian War). Plato was contemporaneous with Lysias and preceded Demosthenes and Hyperides. And Plato too composed a funeral oration for those who had died in the war against Corinth. However, unlike these orators and Thucydides, Plato did not set out

12. See Loraux, 1986.

to praise the bravery of the Athenian democracy. If the *Menexenus* can rightly be called a political—and possibly even a funeral—oration, that is simply because it is a pamphleteering pastiche directed against the Athenian democracy.

The *Menexenus*, possibly written later than the *Gorgias*,[13] continues the critique of rhetoric launched in the latter, concentrating in particular on 'the kind of persuasion . . . that rhetoric creates in law courts or any public meeting' (*Gorgias*, 454e7–8). Again Plato denounces political eloquence, the demagogic mode of discourse favoured by the Athenian democracy. In the *Gorgias*, the critique of the use of both flattery and lying as tools of government was both ethical (the mode of life favoured by rhetoric is opposed to the philosophical life, and is condemned) and also political (the orators who govern Athens have never improved their co-citizens e.g. 515c–517a). But in the *Gorgias*, Socrates did not appeal to Athenian history, at least never in order to establish or justify any of his critical arguments. Historical events were neglected in favour of an examination of the modes of life that politicians aim to impose upon the citizens. The *Menexenus* now reinforced the Athenian (anti-democratic) theme of the *Gorgias*' critique by using historical material, namely the most famous elements in the catalogue of Athenian triumphs.

The funeral oration that Socrates addresses to Menexenus, as he leaves the Council, is devoted to praising the Athenians who died in the war against Corinth (which lasted from 395 until the peace of 386). As was required by the genre of the *epitaphios*, the orator praises the heroism of the fighters who died for the city by associating them with those who were

---

13. The *Menexenus* refers to the Peace of Antalcidas (387/6) but not to any later events, so its date is estimated to be 386. This makes it undoubtedly one of the dialogues that coincided with Plato's 'return' to Athens and the foundation of his Academy which, as this pastiche shows, is inseparable from his own political commitment.

once their ancestors. The speech thus traces the history of the valour of Athenian heroes from the time of legendary conflicts right down to the recent occasion of mourning that forms the main subject of the speech. If we regard the oration attributed to Lysias[14] as the model for this genre and agree that the pastiche constituted by the *Menexenus* follows the rules so set out,[15] we can see that this glorious Athenian history is assigned a twofold beginning. The first is the legendary beginning, starting with the ancestor's victory over the Amazons and the help that Theseus brought to Adrastus;[16] the second beginning is that of the Persian Wars.[17] Those two triumphs are identical in the sense that they simultaneously establish and legitimate Athenian hegemony. Athens is consecrated as the home of an autochthonous people,[18] the Athenians as humans born from the earth which nourished them and then made them the friends of the gods. Also, these Athenians—apparently from the very beginning—have always lived under a political regime based on common interests and common justice.[19]

14. The oration of the pseudo-Lysias was, of course, later than Pericles' oration, the first known example of the genre, which may have been delivered in 431. This *Funeral Oration* will from now on be cited as a text by Lysias, despite the probability that he was not, in fact, its author.

15. The subsequent history of the *Menexenus* is, to put it mildly, paradoxical. For a long time it was regarded as the most successful of all orations on this theme and also as authentic (and sincere). The testimony and misunderstanding of Dionysius of Halicarnassus (*c.*60–*c.*8BC) are edifying. Dionysius studied the *Menexenus*, praising its overall quality, but strongly criticized passages that he judged to be too heavy or discordant and thus to mar its excellence (*Demosthenes*, 5–7 and 23–30; also On *Literary Composition*, 9 and 18).

16. Lysias, *Funeral Oration*, 4–10.

17. *Id.*, 20–53.

18. *Id.*, 17; *Menexenus*, 237b6.

19. Lysias speaks of 'democracy' (18), whereas Socrates (or Aspasia) is less bothered about terminology but is more precise about the nature of the government: 'It is in very truth an "aristocracy", backed by popular approbation' (*Menexenus*, 238d1–2), as this combines political equality and equality of birth (*isonomia* and *isogonia*).

Funeral orations provide democratic propaganda with historical evidence of this Athenian excellence.

What is peculiar to these orations is that the ancient legends and the more recent events all offer the same message. This is that democracy is the excellent regime which, from the earliest beginnings, has always guaranteed Athens' triumph over barbarians and hegemony over the other Greek cities which, without Athens, would be as orphans sold into slavery. However, mention of the Persian Wars and later Athenian exploits should not obscure the discontinuous nature of the historical account. As Loraux stresses, the Athenian orators present:

> the history of Athens within a temporal space that is far more extended than that of the historiographers, not even bothering to fill in the gaps as the authors of chronological accounts do, because the everlasting nature of Athenian merit itself ensures the coherence of their accounts. So, in the historical *excursus* of a funeral oration, we do not find the unfolding of a continuous sequence, but, instead, the repetitive and exemplary staging of one and the same *aretê*.[20]

Funeral orations are content to pick out brave deeds from the flow of a historical or legendary sequence of events already familiar to their public, without bothering to justify the tools or procedures used to link the past with the present. Their concern is thus not at all historiographical, nor even historical, since the facts that they recall must always be sufficiently well-known for the speech to need to do no more than allude to them. All that the funeral orations add is the emphasis of praise: an oration sets out to convey whatever Athenian history may not establish firmly enough—such as the excellence of Athens. It thus operates as an exhortation, seeking to get the living 'to imitate the virtue of those men'

20. Loraux, 1986, pp. 155–56.

(236e6). The chronology of the heroic exploits is therefore only relatively important and the catalogue of the exploits takes second place to the rhetorical presentation of the excellence of Athens—to such a point, indeed, that Pericles can deliver his funeral speech without even feeling obliged to refer to Athenian history to illustrate his praise.[21] As Loraux, again, remarks, the funeral oration treats the past as a litany of 'selected excerpts', rejecting the work of enquiry to which historiography had been devoted since the beginning of the fifth century.[22] Its sole purpose is to sing the praises of Athenian democracy, in Athens. History is simply the source on which the orators can draw for the exploits that they commemorate.

Lysias' *Funeral Oration* and the one attributed to Pericles (Thucydides, II, 60–4) are the focus of Plato's pastiche, which differs from them on a number of points with respect to its legendary and historical material. Those differences, which clearly give the pastiche its meaning, in the first place affect the scope of the material. As noted above, in Thucydides there is no historical material at all; and what there is in Lysias' oration is treated quite differently in the *Menexenus*, for the orator Socrates pays hardly any attention to legendary exploits and totally neglects the episode of the Amazons and that of the Heraclidae.[23] Apart from the initial

21. *The History of the Peloponnesian War*, II, 34–46 (on this absence of exploits see Loraux, op. cit., p. 163). Socrates reveals that the oration delivered by Pericles was composed by his Milesian wife Aspasia (236b5–6); they are thus both by the same author. The remark clearly suggests that the *Menexenus* should be considered as a critique of Thucydides' version of the reign of Pericles.

22. Loraux, op. cit. pp. 165–66.

23. Socrates merely alludes to this, at 239c2–3. In his *Rhetoric*, Aristotle points out that the aid given to the Heraclidae and the Battle of Marathon are the two premisses for the oratorical, or political, syllogism designed to incite the Athenians either to go to war or not (II, 22, 1396a). That is quite a telling remark, for it confirms that a funeral oration was always delivered at the end of a conflict but also, more importantly, on the eve of another, for which it exhorted the citizens to prepare.

emphasis placed on autochthony, Plato seems to favour only the historical chronology that begins with the Persian Wars. It is the full treatment given to this recent period that distinguishes the *Menexenus* from Lysias' speech, for the *Menexenus* dwells upon the Peloponnesian War, while this is, understandably, omitted by the democratic orator. The other, less obvious, differences concern the respective political messages that the two speeches draw from the exploits of the past. To help us to identify these and to appreciate them fully, here is a plan of the speech of Socrates/Aspasia:

234a1–236d3: Prologue
  234c1–235c6: the charm of the funeral oration
  235e8–236d3: Aspasia
236d4–249c8: the oration
    236d4–237b2: justification and plan of the oration (birth/education/exploits)
    237b3–237e2: good birth (autochthony and the gods' love)
    237e2–238b6: nurture and education
    238b7–239a5: the political constitution
  239a6–246a4: the Athenian exploits
    239a6–239c3: the legendary exploits
    239c3–241e5: the Persian Wars
      239d1–240a4: the Persian empire
      240a5–240e6: Marathon
      240e7–241c4: Salamis and Artemision
      241c5–241e5: Plataea
    241e6–243d7: the three wars against Greeks
      242a6–242c2: Tanagra
      242c3–242e4: Sphacteria
      242e5–243d7: the Sicilian expedition
    243e1–244b3: the civil war
    244b4–246a4: the Corinthian War
  246a5–246c8: presentation of the oration
  246d1–248d6: imaginary speech by the dead

[19]

248d7–249c8: exhortation and consolation
249d1–249e7: epilogue

The chronology of the Platonic oration covers an extremely vast period. It stretches from Darius' second expedition against Greece (490)[24] down to the peace of Antalcidas (386),[25] so that Socrates recalls and glorifies more than a century of exploits. The historical part of his speech begins with the battle of Marathon, as in the other orations.[26] Then come all the themes characteristic of such speeches: autochthony, praise of the constitution, the initial glory and exemplary valour embodied by the exploits against the Great King, the hegemony of Athens and its status as the devoted champion of liberty. The arrangement of these themes also conforms to custom, which always has the praise of the dead followed by consolation for the living.

The stylistic figures introduced in the course of the carefully composed plan (which, moreover, follows the introduction faithfully) testify to Plato's desire to exploit all the resources of the genre and to conform to all its formal constraints. This is crucial for the success of the pastiche, which really only turns into satire at the point when one comes to appreciate its treatment of the exploits of the past and the conclusions that these inspire in the orator.

As mentioned above, the historical account of the exploits occupies an important place in the Platonic oration. This is the specific feature of the *Menexenus* that distinguishes it from the other orations, not only that of Thucydides, which ignores the chronology altogether, but also that of Lysias. Commentators on the *Menexenus* bring out the similarity of the two texts and underline how strongly Plato's dialogue is

24. The *Menexenus* refers to this expedition, led by the Persian Datis (240a); see Herodotus, VI, 94 f.
25. Socrates alludes to this at 245e.
26. Lysias, 23 f. And Thucydides also alludes to this as the first act of bravery (*History of the Peloponnesian War*, II, 39, 5).

inspired by Lysias' oration, which must have been delivered only a few years before the peace of Antalcidas (386). But, although they successfully establish the similarity in themes and structure, they ignore the fact that in Lysias' oration the historical material, with its catalogue of exploits, takes up less of the speech and does not receive the meticulous attention that Socrates devotes to it. The first example, that of Marathon, shows this clearly. Where Lysias recalls that the king of Persia 'despatched against us [the Athenians] an army of five hundred thousand men' (21), whose advance was blocked solely by the Athenians, who then went on to win the battle of Marathon, Plato produces a far more detailed historical account (240a5–240e7). Drawing his information from Herodotus, he explains that the Persian expedition was directed not only against Athens but also Eretria, and that it was composed of five hundred thousand men plus three hundred ships, under the command of Datis.[27] Plato also notes that the Persians first disembarked on Eretrian soil and then made their way to Marathon. There the Athenians, unaided, won the day, but they were, nevertheless, eventually joined by the Spartans. Whereas Lysias' praise clearly tends to give all the credit to the Athenians, in general the historical detail provided by Plato presents Marathon as a conflict that involved several cities (Eretria and Sparta, as well as Athens), all of which were saved by Athens.

The first effect of this kind of historiographical scrupulousness—backed by the authority of the historians—is to counter the exclusively Athenian interpretation of the battle. But it is also characteristic of the most remarkable feature of the composition of the *Menexenus*. Plato's oration is not content simply to produce a sequence of Athenian exploits: it draws from historical chronology a type of continuity that is absent from Lysias' *Funeral Oration*. In

27. Herodotus provides the same information but gives different figures, see VI, 94–120.

Lysias' speech, the various sequences are linked together by interventions on the part of the orator. In drawing attention to the 'selected excerpts' nature of the examples of bravery in the *Funeral Oration*, Loraux points out the frequency with which phrases such as *meta tauta* ('after which', 'following which') are used and also points out that the speech enumerates the wars that it lists one after the other.[28] But those selected excerpts or sequences are also introduced by transitional links. Lysias himself intervenes in the course of his speech, which piles on references and questions to his addressees as well as references to the fact that they all belong to one and the same community (the ancient heroes, the orator himself, and his public are all included, like kin, in the praise). The *Menexenus* similarly exploits its assertive function but does so more discreetly in that it does not attempt to provide links between the historical sequences. The account is continuous, evoking Tanagra and the conflicts of 461–455 following the victory of Plataea (242c3, *meta tauta*). Nor is it interrupted when, one page further on, Socrates has the civil war (in Piraeus, 243e1, here again, *meta tauta* . . .) follow on after the Scilian expedition.

Plato thus produces a funeral oration that appears to be more concerned with history and accuracy than those that preceded it. Naturally, the Peloponnesian War, ignored by Lysias,[29] attracts more attention. But it is not a matter simply of that war. The material as a whole is treated in an original fashion, since Socrates records all the facts concerning the Athenian wars, linking them together one after another. From the point of view of historical exactitude, the *Menexenus* comprises a large number of omissions and silences or compromises, all of which enhance the praise of Athens and, as the genre of the funeral oration demands, the

28. Loraux, op. cit., p. 155. But, as needs to be emphasized, only the *Menexenus* lists the wars.
29. It disappears between paragraphs 57 and 58 of the *Funeral Oration*, with no explanation given.

dialogue provides a catalogue of exploits favourable to the city's hegemony. But, contrary to the genre of which it is a pastiche, it lists the Athenian exploits in such a way that, instead of being a catalogue of repeated instances of Athenian excellence, it becomes the history of a decline. Loraux detected a link between the *meta tauta* of the *Oration*'s selected excerpts and the *Menexenus*' 'enumeration' of the Athenian wars. But this enumeration does not *count* the Athenian victories; rather, it *classifies* them in the decreasing order of a continuous hierarchy. The plan of Plato's oration is not that of a list, but rather of a hierarchical classification which allots the 'first prize' (240e7) to the victory of Marathon and the second (241a1) to Salamis and Artemision, so that, contrary to the principle of a funeral oration, Plato introduces differences of value between the various exploits.[30]

The differences become increasingly marked, as can be seen when considering the succession of the six conflicts. Marathon pitted Athens, alone, against the huge barbarian army. Next, the battles of Salamis and Artemision at sea 'completed' (241a6) the land victory of Marathon. Then came Plataea, 'the third in number and in excellence' (241c5–6), which sealed definitively victory over the Great King and the salvation of Greece, 'this time for both the Spartans and the Athenians' (241c6–7). With this third victory in the Persian Wars, merit is divided between the Greeks and, as Socrates insists, it merely rounds off the

30. This oration, like those of Lysias and Thucydides, picks out exploits of exceptional, unparalleled value: those of the Battle of Marathon. This explains why democratic heroism traced back to Marathon, and this serves as a model for subsequent exploits (see Thucydides, II, 34, 5: 'The coffins are laid in the public sepulchre, which is situated in the most beautiful suburb of the city; there they always bury those fallen in war, except indeed those who fell at Marathon; for their valour the Athenians judged to be pre-eminent and they buried them on the spot where they fell'. But the exploits of Marathon are not classified according to their value, since it is precisely their everlasting merit that the oration is designed to establish).

first two exploits (241d5). From Marathon to Plataea, the excellence thus diminishes, or is shared, and the enemy becomes less daunting. This trend continues through the following three conflicts, in which the Athenians are opposed by other Greeks. First come Tanagra and Oenophyta, which are sparked off by rivalry and envy (242a3–5), then the victory over Sparta at Sphacteria, and finally the third war: the Sicilian expedition. This second set of exploits thus shows the Greeks tearing one another apart for mistaken reasons and shows Athens little by little coming to oppose all the other Greeks. At Tanagra, and then at Oenophyta, the Athenians clash with the Spartans to save the liberty of the Boeotians; in other words, they defend 'Greek liberty against the Greeks' (242b6–7). History then develops this strange paradox further for, just a few years later, the Athenians are at war with 'the rest of Greece' (242e2) and eventually find themselves opposed 'to all the Greeks and the barbarians' (243b7), that is to say against the whole world of human beings (*pantôn anthrôpôn*, 243d3–4). From the time of Marathon to that of the Sicilian expedition, Athens preserves a hegemony which, initially embracing just her Greek allies, later comes to encompass the entire world. After fighting the barbarians and the Greeks, Athens, finding no more enemies that measure up, makes peace and settles down to fight itself (this is the civil war in which the people of Eleusis clash with those of Piraeus). Then the more recent past is evoked and Socrates recalls how Athens, wishing to recover her legitimate hegemony, her fleet and her walls, had once again to confront on her own a Greek-barbarian alliance (in the war against Corinth) on her own.

According to the *Menexenus*, between 490 and 386 Athens underwent a quadruple evolution. First, owing to the mediocrity, jealousy and defection of her allies, Athens found herself increasingly isolated; or rather, she moved from one kind of isolation into another. She fought alone for the liberty of the whole of Greece, which recognized her hegemony, then found herself confronting the whole world, which was challenging it. Secondly, and this constituted the major aspect of that challenge, following Marathon she immediately acquired a hegemony over the sea, which she strove (successfully) to defend right down to the war against Corinth ('We still retained our ships, our walls, and our own colonies when we ceased from the war — so welcome to our enemies also was its cessation', 245e4–7). From being a land-based power confronting the barbarian fleet that disembarked close to Marathon, at the beginning of the fourth century, she became a hegemonic maritime power. Thirdly, even as she multiplied her exploits, Athens came to experience dissension, first among the Greeks, when jealousy split them apart so seriously that some rallied to the barbarians and rose up against Athens, and then within her own bosom, when she was afflicted by civil war (242e1 and 243e3). Fourthly and lastly, this descent into solitude and dissension was accompanied by psychological and moral troubles and aggravations. At first these took the form of rivalry and envy, which set the other Greeks against the Athenians as early as the end of the Persian Wars (the rivalry and envy are contrasted to the goodness of the Athenians, 242b7), and these were aggravated by the indignity and injustice of the behaviour of those other Greeks.[31] Then they took the more convoluted form of internal divisions in Athens itself. However, the *Menexenus* adds, 'It was not through wickedness that they set upon one another, nor yet through hatred, but through misfortune' (244a7).

With its account of these four forms of historical evolution, the *Menexenus* distinguishes itself from the traditional catalogues of the funeral oration sufficiently clearly for the reader soon to realize that it is a pastiche of the form and themes of the latter and is designed to support an argument that is in every respect opposed to democratic praise of Athens. It is remarkable that it is with the aid of a historical

---

31. See all the comments that contrast Athenian justice to the churlish unfairness of other Greeks: at 242c5, 243a2, 243b3 f and 243c6 f.

account, the kind from which other funeral orations borrowed their snippets of bravery, and by fashioning it as freely as other orators did, that Plato manages to subvert the genre to the point of getting it to contradict itself entirely, as if it were a refutation.

The many historical interpretations and the chronological omissions or inversions contained in the *Menexenus* show that the historical development of Athenian valour should be read as a chronicle of decadence. So Socrates' speech is in fact a travesty of the genre of the funeral oration, and undermines both its form and its traditional historical message. We have already seen that the *Menexenus*, far from repeating a single exploit, recounts Athens' evolution, an evolution that sinks ever lower but that, nevertheless, successfully accomodates the usual democratic propaganda and retains the image of Athens left to stand on her own against barbarians and others who are envious of her. But if Athens is depicted as finding herself alone, that is precisely because the *Menexenus* intends to make her responsible for her own disappearance. We should, therefore, pay attention to the fact that Plato's pastiche modifies certain of the conventions of the funeral oration, and does so in order to make it acknowledge what the genre is usually designed to conceal. This is that Athens, as a result of her wars against the other Greeks and the internal conflicts she has experienced, now finds herself in the very worst and most dishonourable of situations, the very state that Lysias, (contradicting the *Funeral Oration* that is attributed to him), deplores in his *Olympic Speech*.

The fact that the *Menexenus* really does replace the usual project of a funeral oration by an account of Athenian decadence is made manifestly clear by a number of expressions associated with the theme of discord, expressions which were, precisely, used at the time of the peace of Antalcidas to refer to the scuppering of Athens. *Stasis* was not only the technical term used in the *Republic* to designate the gravest of evils by which a city can be afflicted. It was

[26]

common generally in political discourse, which was already using it as the gravest and most indubitable sign of dissolution in a city. In the *Olympic Speech*, contemporaneous with the *Menexenus*,[32] Lysias, far from praising the hegemony of Athens, laments her deplorable situation and appeals to his co-citizens to turn, instead, against Dionysius of Syracuse or the Spartans. In order to denounce the iniquity of these false allies, Lysias sketches a rapid portrait of Athens and her 'shameful plight' (para. 4). He does this using exactly the same terms as the *Menexenus*, dwelling upon the conflicts in which Athens has been the victim or dupe. Those conflicts have been of three kinds: either wars (lost against the barbarians) (para. 3), or wars between Greek cities (para. 4 and para. 9), or internal clashes within Athens (para. 4). In the downward spiral of troubles, three terms recur: war (*polemos*), inter-city quarrelling (*philoneikia*), and internal strife (*stasis*). In both the *Menexenus* and the *Olympic Speech*, those three terms denote progressively worsening situations.[33]

As Lysias sees it, the worst aspect of these conflicts is their historical outcome: the enslavement of part of the Athenian territory and the hegemony of the Spartans, now 'the leaders of the Greeks' (para. 8), the Spartans who now possess what the *Funeral Oration* attributed to Athens, namely maritime power ('You know the empire is for those who command the sea', (para. 5), the role of 'the saviours of Greece in her past dangers', (para. 7), and the fame of citizens who 'have their dwelling places unravaged through unwalled and, strangers to faction and defeat, observe always the same rules of life' (ibid.). This picture, which is much sharper than a funeral oration could be, leads ato an exhortation in which Lysias

32. Bizos, 1926, dates the speech to the years following the Peace of Antalcidas, and inclines to favour the Olympiad of 384 (*Discours*, II, p. 201).
33. In the *Menexenus*, the transition from war to quarrelling among the Greeks thus occurs when jealousy and envy rear their heads (234b1 f).

asks the Athenians to 'feel shame for past events and fear for those that lie in the future, and to compete with [our] ancestors, by whom the foreigner, in grasping at the land of others, was deprived of his own, and who expelled the despots and established freedom for all in common' (para. 6). Although this speech still smacks of democratic propaganda (the hegemony of Athens is claimed as a due that has been stolen by Sparta), it is by no means devoted to the praise of Athens. The excellence of past exploits has been interrupted (which is quite contrary to Lysias' funeral oration, which glorified the continued repetition of this excellence), and it is very much to be feared that the Athenians will never manage to recover it.

The contrast between the *Funeral Oration* and the *Olympic Speech* helps us to see how Plato's pastiche, going against all the rules of the genre, replaces the Athenian exploits within a historical analysis couched in terms of a critical diagnosis of the fall of Athens. The funeral oration is in this way subverted by the vocabulary and by a chronological schema used to condemn Athens.

In similar fashion, the *Menexenus* calls into question the funeral speech delivered by Pericles in *The History of the Peloponnesian War (II*, 60–4) — all the more so, probably, since Socrates presents his speech as forming part of that earlier funeral speech, or even as its continuation (236b6). Thucydides' version stresses the often repeated and the constant features of the funeral oration, which has thus remained unaltered from the first year of the Peloponnsian War right down to the peace of Antalcidas.[34] It is as though, as the funeral oration certainly sets out to demonstrate, Athenian merit had by no means diminished between the former date and the latter. As we have seen, the *Menexenus*

34. The flagrant anachronism (Socrates claims to have heard Aspasia 'yesterday', 236b1 f.) again underlines the link between the *Menexenus* and the oration in Thucydides — the more so, perhaps, in that, in a way, Aspasia was herself a victim of the Athenian democracy.

contradicts the perennial nature of Athens' greatness by its account of her fall. The initial presentation of this funeral oration itself indicates this clearly enough, as it suggests that Socrates' speech may consist of a collection of passages left over from the earlier funeral oration (236b6). This collection, put together by Aspasia, is thus composed either of pieces of the speech which Pericles did not deliver at the time, or else of passages remaining from the speech that he did indeed deliver and that was considerably longer than is suggested by Thucydides. In either case, the satirical intention is the same, since the 'left-over' bits that Socrates pronounces contradict Pericles' funeral oration.

This is so, in particular, as regards the presentation of the continuity in merit and liberty among the Athenians, with which Pericles introduces his speech (II, 36, 1–2). Pericles evokes the memory of the ancestors and praises them for having bequeathed to the generations that followed them a city that was free, self-sufficient, and endowed with its original constitution (37, 1) and with good and respected laws. The valour of the Athenians matches their taste for beauty and knowledge and their disinterested goodwill. The main interest of this speech certainly lies in its political, or constitutional, aspect. It is Athens' constitution, which is inseparable from the eternal value of its citizens, that ensures the city's greatness and strength. This point is all the more important given that the *Menexenus*, despite neglecting the question of the political system (to which it refers only by remarking, vaguely and allusively, that the present-day regime is the same as that of the past, whether people call it an aristocracy or a democracy), on several occasions describes the ethical nature of the city and its citizens. In doing so, it deplores the lack of qualities that Pericles praised. Whereas Pericles paid homage to Athenian justice and goodwill, underlining his fellow-citizens' absence of anger and their enemies' lack of irritation or resentment,[35]

35. *Aganaktêsis*, 41, 3.

[29]

Socrates stresses the negative sentiments that are gradually changing the Athenian character for the worse. In the *Menexenus*, irritation is not associated with the enemies that Athens has vanquished; rather, it is the sentiment that the Athenians themselves feel, faced as they are with the ingratitude of the other Greeks (244b7), an ingratitude all the more dangerous given that it is accompanied by jealousy and envy.

Here again, the history related in the *Menexenus* counteracts the objectives and messages of the traditional oration, and does so in order to make them the object of a political critique that deplores the falseness of the memories that the imperialist democracy allows itself. When we compare the *Menexenus* both to Lysias' *Funeral Oration* and to Pericles' speech, it is possible to distinguish three major criticisms. Each calls into question a particular aspect of the democratic representation of Athens, and does so on the basis of a past historical event or episode.

In the first place, the *Menexenus* considers the history of Athens from the time of Marathon onwards, as the development of a single city, which starts off united but soon becomes divided. The funeral orations always represent Athens as a united and perfectly homogeneous city: the character of its citizens is unique and common to all, and Athenian excellence is all the more continuous because it is incomparable. In some unexplained way, the city and its citizens possess qualities peculiar to them alone, and will do so forever.[36] It is the constitution that gives the city its unity, and it is identified with their virtue: Athens is a democracy and its citizens are free men.[37] Democratic unity rests upon the *isonomia* ('equality in law') and shared

36. A particular feature of the myth of autochthony, when used to combine the ideas of *isogonia* and *isonomia* (equality in birth and equality in law), is that it founds Athenian political excellence *in nature*.

37. *History of the Peloponnesian War*, II, 37, 1–2; *Funeral Oration*, 18.

interests of the citizens.[38] It is that freedom and those shared interests that account for Athenian bravery in moments of peril. The funeral oration thus depicts a united and constant city, never confusing its destiny with those of other Greek cities. It is worth pointing out that the fate of the other Greeks is never completely confused with that of Athens and that, even in the midst of its leagues and alliances, Athens always preserves her hegemonic status. Athens is always the hero of Greece or even, as both Pericles and Lysias claim, its 'model'; Athens always retains her exceptional individuality, whatever enemy she faces, whether barbarian or Greek. At the price of a paradox so forced as to be comical, the *Menexenus* for its part shows that the city has never known a defeat (except as a result of her own dissensions: 'In truth, it was by our own dissensions that we were brought down and not by the hands of other men', 243d6–7). But this paradox, which changes all military conflicts into civil war, makes the funeral oration recognize the discord that gradually comes to trouble the city.[39] This is, perhaps, the major criticism that Plato's pastiche levels at the history of Greek democracy: the idea that a city with a democratic constitution can be unified is contradicted by the Athenian conflicts past and present.

Secondly, the *Menexenus* draws attention to these political dissensions in psychological and ethical terms that call into question the value of the citizens and the greatness of the Athenian character. This critique stems from the previous one, as it again shows that interests, far from being common and shared, are opposed and give rise to every possible form of discord. But this critique is also original in that it lays emphasis on individual character traits associated with

38. *History of the Peloponnesian War*, II, 40, 5; *Funeral Oration*, ibid.
39. As has been noted above, when comparing the *Menexenus* to the *Funeral Oration*.

the passions (jealousy,[40] rivalry, resentment, envy). Both Thucydides and the author of the *Funeral Oration* associate the Athenian hegemony with democratic liberty, at the price of drawing a clear distinction between the private occupations of citizens and their participation in public responsibilities.[41] In their view, the distinctive feature of the democratic regime lies in the perfect appropriateness of those two forms of activity, ensured by respect for the law.[42] The identity of individual characteristics and sentiments and the value of the city thus depends on two conditions: respect for the law and warrior courage (whether this be *aretê* in general or the more specific expression of warrior courage, *andreia*).[43] The *Menexenus* picks up both terms of this comparison, but subjects each to a similar shift. Before evoking the memory of the Persian Wars, Socrates remarks:

> We and our people, on the contrary, being all born of one mother, claim to be neither the slaves of one another nor the masters; rather the equality of our origin (*isogonia*) naturally makes us seek equality in law (*isonomia*), and to yield to one another in no respect save in reputation for virtue and understanding' (239a1–5).

In the *Republic*, *isogonia* was to be described as a purely political *lie*, designed to favour the community of guardians

40. Jealousy is the subject of a comprehensive study by Brisson, 1996, pp. 41–59. He refers to the *Menexenus* and shows how jealousy, a hybrid psychological form of pleasure and pain, has the peculiar power to engender ignorance and tyranny (which is its political consequence). It can thus be regarded as 'the motivating force in the darkest side to history: war between States, civil war, murder, violence, and theft and conflict of every kind'.

41. Pericles frequently stresses the private, domestic, liberty of the citizens (in particular at 37, 2; 40, 2; and 41, 1).

42. Respect that is inseparable from isonomia. See *The History of the Peloponnesian War*, II, 37 and the *Funeral Oration*, 19.

43. See in particular *The History of the Peloponnesian War*, II, 39 and 42; *Funeral Oration*, 20.

by getting them all to believe that they were born from the earth, the same earth (III, 414d–415d). Democracy bases *isonomia* on this fiction; and, Socrates insists, it does so by giving power to the man or men who are judged to be virtuous and wise because that is what they seem to be. A few lines earlier, Socrates had defined the democratic regime as follows: 'the man that is deemed to be wise or good rules and governs' (238d7–8). That definition is informed by two contradictions that arise out of the Platonic critique. The first stems from the legendary foundations of the law, which derives political equality from a mythical (and false) *isogonia*. The second stems from the very institution of political *isonomia*, which is certainly not guaranteed by a democratic constitution that 'is, in very truth, an "aristocracy" backed by popular approbation' (238d1).[44] This hybrid constitution, which right from the start contradicts its mythical origin, thus rests upon a type of reputation that will soon run counter to *isonomia*, since the crowd gives responsibilites and power to those who seem to be the best men (238d4–5). In this way, the *Menexenus*, by always insisting upon the fact that the virtue of government rests simply upon the opinion of the crowd, suggests that *isonomia* is contradicted by the exercise of power. It is as though Athens would not allow itself to choose between an aristocracy and a democracy.

The critique attacks the unified and egalitarian representation of the city given by funeral orations. But also, in the last analysis, it simply repeats the contrary diagnosis offered, as we have seen, by Lysias' *Olympic Speech* but, even before that, and above all, by Pericles too, whose speeches by no means always testify to the political equality of the city or the common exercise of power. In Book II of the *History of*

---

44. On the notion of *isonomia*, its status in the democratic ideology and its various Platonic interpretations, see Vlastos, 1953, pp. 337–66; and Joly, 1985, pp. 312 f.

the Peloponnesian War, Pericles responds to the Athenian discontent (caused by the successive defeats and the plague epidemic) by trying to justify the continuation of the war. He starts by reminding his listeners that the strength of the city and the government are conditions for the safeguarding of private interests (II, 60), and then he praises the military power of Athens, as if to prove the reality of that strength (II, 62). He intends to devote his authority to developing that power and preserving the empire (II, 63–64). Thucydides, who contrasts the moderation of Pericles to the ineffectiveness of the later decisions taken by the Athenians, explains that power was not in the hands of the crowd and, as for Pericles, he 'led them rather than was led by them' (II, 65, 8). The historian then feels obliged to add the following constitutional clarification: 'So Athens, though in name a democracy, gradually became in fact a government ruled by its foremost citizen' (II, 65, 9).[45] This specification of the regime is thus no longer the same as that of the funeral oration, for it now acknowledges that power is not exercised in common, but on the contrary it distinguishes between the governors and the governed in the city. That is precisely what the *Menexenus* points out, showing that the Athenian constitution was an indeterminate mixture, a ferment of discord and dissension. The unity of the city is thus not even recognized by those who rule it, whatever the claims of democratic propaganda. From the point of view later adopted by the analysis in the *Republic*, democracy remains government by public opinion, that is to

45. Thucydides, who was a 'moderate' supporter of democracy, distinguishes between two periods and two points of view that Plato was to seek to merge: in the eyes of the historian, the responsibility of Pericles and that of the Athenians were not identical. He claimed that Pericles favoured a defensive policy for persevering the empire, but the Athenians did not stick to that. Plato, on the contrary, regarded the democratic corruption of the city (for which Pericles carried much of the blame) and belligerent imperialism as inseparable.

say power given over to whoever seems most worthy to exercise it.[46]

The third and final criticism, when comparing the *Menexenus* to Lysias' oration and Pericles' speech, is that Plato's pastiche lays emphasis on the maritime power of Athens. Maritime hegemony is the precondition, recognized and justified by the democrats, of the Athenian empire. The dream of being an island that Pericles wanted to share with his fellow citizens is offset in his funeral oration by a military and imperialistic vision that is its counterpart.[47] For the democratic funeral oration, Athenian power remained synonymous with an empire that Lysias had not yet renounced when he delivered the *Olympic Speech*, after the peace of Antalcidas. The *Menexenus* links the expansion of the fleet and the development of maritime conflicts with the isolation of Athens; thus, the critique links, as contemporary events, the progressive deterioration of the city, the increase in dissent and the development of maritime warfare.

46. The political rule of public opinion, or the apparent and generally approved power of the governors appointed by it, is condemned in the *Gorgias* and in the *Republic* as being a rule of demagogy and ignorance. Plato's most explicit and severe criticisms are to be found in the *Gorgias*, 502e–503d, and the *Republic*, VIII, 557a–563d. But what the *Menexenus* and the *Republic* chiefly denounce are political contradictions. This is the first indication that Plato is not content to reject democracy as a bad regime, on the basis of (what is sometimes alleged to be) his support for the pro-Spartan conservative circles. On the contrary, and the qualification seems to me to be crucial, it is in *the name of the democratic constitution* that Plato condemns the unequal exercise of power. It is never the people as a whole who are condemned, but the way in which demagogic rhetoric takes advantage of its ignorance, in order to govern with impunity. Again, what Plato is attacking are the factions in the city, for politics should, on the contrary, produce unity for it. From this point of view, conservative ideology is equally reprehensible since it demands power for the well-born to counter domination by the ignorant mob. What Plato aims to refute is the very idea that the city should accommodate distinct and opposed political interests.
47. *History of the Peloponnesian War*, II, 36, 63–65 (the empire); II, 39 (the open city and the fleet).

Political competence

It could be said of the various political developments proposed in the early 'Socratic' dialogues that they all, in their
different ways, contribute to the elaboration of political
thought, the principal characteristic of which is that it is
anthropological. On the one hand the city is envisaged as a
human individual, with a particular way of behaving, and on
the other it is conceived as the total collection of men that it
contains and has contained in the past. From the latter point
of view, such thinking is not untimely, for Aristotle tells
us that the Athenian city was perceived by its citizens more
as 'a constitutional community among citizens', a certain
relationship instituted between certain people, rather than as
a place, a history, or even a culture. That concept of the city
as a gathering or community of people is never questioned;
and it reappears in the *Republic*. On the other hand, the
nature of the relationships that found and organize the
community with a view to achieving certain ends is something that is much discussed.

The explanation for the 'silence' about politics in the
early dialogues should therefore, as suggested above, not be
sought in (hypothesised) 'moral' ambitions of the character
Socrates. Rather, it is to be found in the subjects and
methods of the research conducted by the early dialogues.
These provide two reasons for that 'silence'.

One has to do with the genre of most of the early
dialogues, each of which is devoted to examining one single
question. Every time, it is a matter of defining a concept or
the nature of something by replying to the question 'what
is X?': what is piety? (*Euthyphron*), what is wisdom?
(*Charmides*), what is a human being? (*Alcibiades I*), what is
courage? (*Laches*), what is friendship? (*Lysis*), etc. These
successive investigations, which adopt the Socratic method of
refutation, are never interested in the city, the constitution,
or the exercise of power as such. Socrates never asks his
interlocuters what the city is, what the nature of the

constitution is, or from what kind of activity or knowledge politics might derive.

The second reason for the silence about politics in these texts—one that is far more important—has to do with the fact that, even if political questions are, to be sure, frequently evoked, it is always purely from the point of view of *knowledge*, which is, precisely, one of the norms, if not the principal norm, that shapes the typical form of a Socratic refutation. For example, in the *Laches*, which examines the nature of courage, that is to say the part of virtue that concerns apprenticeship for armed combat, courage is defined by and based on the possession of a certain kind of knowledge.[48] The fact that courage may have political effects and opportunities is less important than pointing out the primacy of knowledge, which makes this particular virtue possible. The same pattern is followed in the other early dialogues that examine the various 'parts of virtue'.[49]

It is always, above all, the possession of some kind of knowledge that gives virtue its status (ethical excellence *is* a cognitive excellence) and important. In short, we may consider all the Socratic dialogues as opportunities to make one and the same point: excellence, whatever the domain in which it is exercised, always depends upon a pre-existing knowledge; virtue, all forms of virtue, must be founded upon knowledge of some kind (*Laches*, 190a–e). One comes to

48. *Laches*, 194d9 f. This definition of courage, produced by Nicias, is still provisional and incomplete. But the definition of virtue through knowledge is retained right up to the end of the dialogue, which can make no further progress.

49. *Laches*, 190c8 and 190d3. The *Laches* provides the opportunity for a critical and methodological explanation of the very structure of the early dialogues. Here, Socrates distinguishes between two kinds of enquiry, one concerning virtue as a whole, the other one of its parts ('What you now describe, Nicias, will be not a part but the whole of virtue', 199e4–5). Every specific study demands but defers a definition of the kind of excellence in question. That is why the specific enquiries can never lead to a conclusion. On the method of enquiry in the early dialogues, see Benson, 2000, and Matthews, 1999. On the *Laches*, see Schmid, 1992.

realize that the term 'virtue' does not only qualify excellence of character or conduct in particular circumstances and that Plato gives it a new, wider meaning by extending it to all activities, whatever they may be. Whereas Greek thought and language had until now restricted virtue to nobility of conduct and character (*êthos*), particularly in the category of warrior courage, Plato extends it beyond the limits of that aristocratic morality, to designate the perfection of any action or activity. In a sense that is as different from its traditional Athenian meaning as it is from our own (for us, virtue is of a moral order and qualifies good conduct), virtue is something that is well done. Also, as we shall see in the *Republic*, the thing that is well done may just as well be a courageous action as fine timber work. We should note that the shift and modification of the common notion of virtue transform it into a concept (excellence)[50] that Plato will put to technical use and that they also make it possible for the philosopher to move into the domain of what, in Athens, was the principal preserve of the garrulous teachers who claimed, precisely, to 'teach virtue' in such a way that their pupils learnt how to run their households and govern their city.[51] If virtue (transformed into excellence) presupposes knowledge, simply to ask the sophists what kind of knowledge they possess and dispense should be enough to lead them into contradiction and discredit.[52]

The demand to base excellence upon some kind of

50. 'Virtue' is the usual translation for the Greek *aretê*, but I often render it more literally by the term 'excellence', which makes it clearer that it is not just a matter of 'morality'. Chapter 2 will return to this point in greater detail.

51. See *Gorgias*, 520e, and the commentary provided by Dodds, 1959 (the most complete and accurate work on this dialogue). See also Kahn, 1983, pp. 75–121.

52. Or clearly, this should have been enough, but the sophists, though greedy, dangerous and ignorant, are clever. Their function in Plato's dialogues deserves fuller examination, for this might show that sophistry is to some extent a Platonic invention.

knowledge, which appears in the *Euthydemus*, the *Meno*, and the *Gorgias*, poses for the first time the question of political competence. Each in turn, these dialogues show that, if such a thing as a specifically political competence exists, it must have a form of excellence, or virtue, and must therefore be based on a form of knowledge: (political) knowledge that must then be the (political) cause of excellence. Of the three dialogues cited above, it is the *Euthydemus* that develops this line of enquiry most fully and comes up with a definition of political knowledge: 'knowledge that benefits us and makes us happy' by making us 'wise and good' (292c1 and 292d6). Socrates recognizes several times that this definition is still unsatisfactory, as it does not account for the political process by which knowledge is conferred, along with goodness, upon the whole group of citizens. In fact, total precision would require one to be able to define the content of that political knowledge which makes a man politically competent as well as the means by which such knowledge can be made effective, that is to say be transmitted. The *Euthydemus* satisfies neither of those two requirements, but it does express them in terms whose importance is all the more remarkable because these continue to be the terms used in the later political discussions, both in the *Republic*'s description of the excellent constitution and in the *Statesman* which, in a different mode of enquiry, examines the *technique* of a political technician. The questions and requirements of the *Euthydemus* thus begin to feel their way toward a more precise version, or a specification, of the more generalized critique of the early dialogues. From now on, the critique developed by Socrates sets out to give an account of the functioning of institutions and to suggest that they might be reformed. In this respect, the following extract from the *Euthydemus* may be considered as the matrix of later developments, in that it identifies two different ways forward for political critical analysis and debate.

At this point in his investigation, Socrates, talking to

[39]

Crito, sums up the ground covered so far by the conversation, the aim of which has been to discover the kind of knowledge or 'art' whose acquisition can be justified for its own sake (not as the instrument or means of acquiring other knowledge):

> *Soc.* So it seemed clear to us that this was the one [art] we were seeking, and was the cause of right conduct in the state, and precisely as Aeschylus' line expresses, is seated alone at the helm of the city, steering the whole, commanding the whole, and making the whole useful.
>
> *Cri.* And surely your notion was a good one, Socrates?
>
> *Soc.* You shall judge of that, Crito, if you care to hear what befell us thereafter. For later on we reconsidered it somewhat in this manner: Look now, does the monarch's art, that rules over all, produce any effect or not? Certainly it does, we said to one another. Would you say so too, Crito?
>
> *Cri.* I would.
>
> *Soc.* Then what would you say is its effect? For instance, if I were to ask you whether medicine, in ruling over all that comes under its rule, has any effect to show, would you not say: Yes, health?
>
> *Cri.* I would.
>
> *Soc.* And what about your art of agriculture? In ruling over all that comes under its rule, what effect does it produce? Would you not say that it supplies us with food from the earth?
>
> *Cri.* I would.
>
> *Soc.* And what of the monarch's art? In ruling over all that comes under its rule, what does it produce? Perhaps you are not quite ready with the answer.
>
> *Cri.* I am not indeed, Socrates.
>
> *Soc.* Nor were we, Crito; yet this much you know, that if this is really the one [art, technique] we are seeking, it must be beneficial.
>
> *Cri.* Certainly.

Soc. Then surely it must purvey something good?

Cri. Necessarily, Socrates.

Soc. And you know we agreed with each other, Cleinias and I, that nothing can be good but some kind of knowledge.

Cri. Yes, so you told me.

(291c4–292b3).[53]

Political competence is here defined as knowledge: on two counts, for it both presupposes some kind of knowledge (whoever engages in politics must know how to use and direct all the tasks to be performed in the city), and also *produces* some kind of knowledge (by making the citizens knowledgeable). Politics is thus defined by reference to these two kinds of knowledge; and this formulation is one that Plato never seems to give up—that politics is a mode of education (*paideia*), of formative culture.[54] It is this definition of political knowledge, synonymous with virtue that is the product of education, that allows the *Meno* and the *Gorgias* to discredit the positions of the democrats and the sophists. These both favour a regime based upon ignorance (which denies the existence of a specifically political knowledge) and one which is also a cause of ignorance (as it shows itself to be incapable of improving the citizens).[55]

The *Meno*, in its turn, develops a similar argument, in

53. This translation, by W.R.M. Lamb (Loeb Classical Library, 1966), is slightly modified.

54. Plato is here returning to a traditional theme (for the Greeks, education is the principle of citizenship: the citizen, a mature man, is an educated, fully developed adult) and Plato renders this theme exceptionally forceful when he declares that any kind of private education must be ruled out. The task of educating all its citizens falls to the city.

55. On this 'double' ignorance, see *Gorgias*, 458e f., which represents the orator before the democratic assembly as an ignoramus addressing a bunch of others like him. See also my introductory remarks in Pradeau, 1997e.

which Socrates describes the paradoxical and hazardous situation in which a city finds itself, even if it includes a number of men 'good at politics', if it can expect from them no kind of education, since they are incapable of teaching their own virtue (e.g. 92e–93c). The question that gives the measure of this dialogue is the following: can virtue be taught? The reason why Meno and Socrates hasten to give it a political meaning is that the teaching of excellence is precisely how Plato would describe the behaviour of the city. A city is a group of people; and here Socrates' generalized critique becomes more precise (the city is neither just nor good, nor happy, and that is because of its ignorance), and so the city is, by implication, waiting for a politician who is also an educator, a master of virtue.

Until the *Republic*, the early dialogues and political theory venture no further, limiting themselves to the programmatic and expectant hope of the *Meno*: a statesman is needed. That hope and expectation constitute the reverse side to disappointment: a true statesman is needed, and this time not a Pericles. Like the critique that paved the way for them, these dialogues preserve an anthropological concept of the city (what is true for an individual is also true for the city, which is a group of individuals). They also preserve a cognitive and pedagogical definition of politics: the government of a community of men calls for the possession of some kind of knowledge and an ability to use this to educate all its members.

2

The political psychology of the Republic

Plato's *Republic* provides the definitive anthropological and cognitive definition of political competence. Here, the notion is both developed and refined, for the dialogue produces definitions of both the city and the knowledge that takes the city as its object and also presides over its government. Furthermore, that definition of political competence is intertwined with a thread of reflection upon the use that this political technique can make of the city.

The great soul that is the city

It is by way of a comparison, at the beginning of Book II, that the *Republic* comes to adopt the political constitution (*politeia*)[56] as its subject. At II, 368c–369a , Socrates, who is trying to define justice in order to determine what constitutes a just man, compares justice in an individual to justice in the

---

56. The *politeia* is the correct title of Plato's dialogue. On the argument of the *Republic* as a whole, see Pappas, 1995, Sayers, 1999. On the Republic as a political text, see Schofield, 2000, pp. 190–257 and 293–302.

city. This is definitely a comparison, not an analogy,[57] for the individual and the city are identical objects, which differ only in scale and upon which *the same letters* are inscribed, those of the term 'justice'.[58] So this is simply a comparison made between something big and something small and, from the point of view of justice, the difference between the human soul and the city is simply *quantitative* in a strictly anthropological sense (and also in an anthropomorphic one: the city is a large-scale individual). So what applies to the human soul, in respect of what is good, just and true, should also apply to the city, which assembles all those souls in a community. However, this comparison rests upon a doctrinal point that justifies the substitution of the term 'soul' for that of 'individual'. The shift from the one to the other very soon affects the comparison of Book II, without occasioning the slightest surprise on the part of any of the interlocutors. The identification of the human individual with his/her soul is all the more natural and straightforward since it has already been introduced in the earlier dialogues and also right at the beginning of the *Republic*.[59] But in the *Republic*, it is justified on grounds more specifically political than those of the standard association. The comparison is now based on the cognitive nature of political excellence. It is because the state must rest on the authority of knowledge that it can be

57. All the same, as we shall see, Plato later (at the beginning of Book IV) replaces this comparison by an analogy.

58. Justice in an individual must be identical to justice in the city. The comparison has already been announced in Book I, at 351a–352a. It should be distinguished from the passage in the *Statesman* which is a precise echo of it (277d–278c). There, the Stranger defines the paradigm (it is a matter of finding one for politics), using the same grammatical example, but makes it play a quite different role: the aim is to recognize the elements of the alphabet, but in *different* syllables. The paradigm thus assumes that there are 'two combinations' (278b), one of which serves as a paradigm to explain the other. The *Republic*, in contrast, simply proposes the same object, the same combination but on a larger scale.

59. 'The soul is the man', *Alcibiades I*, 130c3. The first book of the *Republic* repeats that definition (at 353d f.).

compared with something that can possess both knowledge and competence: namely the soul. The excellence of the city thus becomes inseparable from the excellence of the thought behind it. It is this, at the very beginning of Book II, that accounts for the arrangement of the citizens into three classes (which are distinguished in the same way as the three kinds of soul). It also accounts for the political status of knowledge (which, through the mediation of the philosopher-rulers or rulers who have become philosophers, must be the source of power in the city).

The emphasis placed, from Plato's earliest dialogues, on knowledge, and the subsequent search for a truly political competence (that is, knowledge) helps to explain the comparison drawn at the beginning of the *Republic*. It is a comparison that deserves all the more attention given that, when it replaces the search for individual justice by a search for political justice, it both gives the dialogue its status as a *Politeia* (a work devoted to the examination of a political constitution) and also provides it with its overall plan. The inclusion of the soul in the comparison is particularly helpful to the exploration of politics as it immediately provides a tripartite object the parts of which can be set out in a hierarchical structure and then unified. Once it is recognized that the city is a large version of the soul, all that needs to be done, notwithstanding a few marginal difficulties, is to make it conform to that pattern.[60] The last part of Book II and all of Books III and IV are devoted to this very task, for they describe the status and function of each of the three groups of citizens.

These three groups are often called 'classes' of citizens,

60. This ploy looks very much like question-begging, or a vicious circle: the conversation, having recognized that there are three types of citizens, at the end of Book IV asks whether there are three types of soul in individuals (and the comparison introduced in Book II reappears: see IV, 434d f.). On the plan of the *Republic* and the principal points that it makes, the most perceptive commentary is also one of the shortest: Brunschwig's article, 1986.

but the term is incorrect. Not only is it anachronistic, but, more importantly, it does not adequately convey Plato's idea that the three groups represent three different species or inclinations of one and the same citizen nature, just as the soul includes three species (without there being three different types of soul).[61] Furthermore, Plato's vocabulary is far from rigid: the groups are said to be three 'kinds', three 'species', three 'races', three 'characters', or even three 'elements'.[62] The soul is said to comprise an intelligent species, an irascible species, and a desiring species, so the city, in its turn, comprises a desiring group (those in the city who produce and exchange things: agricultural cultivators, artisans and traders), an irascible group (the guardians, who must protect the city from enemies both internal and external), and an intelligent group (the philosophers, who love knowledge and who govern). It should be remembered that this division into three functional groups in no way reproduces the other distinctions that affected Athenian citizenship. Citizenship was, in the first place, subject to a preliminary selection (a citizen was not a slave, not a foreigner, not a metic; and a citizen with full rights was neither a woman nor a child). Secondly, it was subject to other reservations, the major criterion being the possession of an (inherited) fortune. Thirdly and finally, the exercise of most responsibilities and magistracies was reserved for those who fulfilled certain census conditions. On top of all this, the

61. For Plato, the soul engages in two activities, thought and movement. Incorporeal, and hence immortal, the soul is a principle of movement which can either set in motion (animate) bodies, or itself enter into contact with other incorporeal realities. These realities, grasped by the intellect, the agent of knowledge, are the 'intelligible Forms' or 'Ideas'. The soul, as the principle of all movement and all knowledge, is what individuates physical objects: when linked to a body, the soul gives life to a living being. For a description of the soul and its functions, see, as well as Book IV of the *Republic*, the *Phaedrus* (245c–249d) and the *Timaeus*, (on the latter, see Pradeau, 1998.
62. A passage in Book IV provides a quite clear idea of this (434c–436b). As will be seen, what gives a group its character is its function.

defence of Athenian society depended not upon a separate military body, a professional army, but upon the obligatory participation of all the citizens. Those who were the most powerful exercised the magistracy of *stratêgos* (as did Pericles, for example) and financed and led an army which the poorer citizens joined, in some cases with all the more alacrity since this was the only employment available to them.[63] At the time when Plato was writing the *Republic*, years after the Peloponnesian War, when this citizen military service was gradually being superseded by mercenary troops, Plato seems to have set out to restore an archaic tripartition (the Indo-European division into three functions: one productive, one military, one priestly) and to set this in opposition to Athenian social classification, and thereby totally transform the distribution of the citizen population.[64] The crucial lever in this transformation had to be the group of guardians, for only their mediating function could relate the productive function to the governing function and was able to provide the force presumably necessary for the exercise of power.

As mentioned above, getting this tripartite grouping of citizens to conform with the equivalent division of types of souls involved no more than marginal difficulties. However, that is not at all what is suggested by the emphatic precautions taken by Socrates, who declares himself to be expecting at any moment the most violent of protests from his interlocutors. The three waves of objection that Socrates says he fears will overwhelm him concern the three most scandalous aspects of the lifestyle of the guardians that is described in Book III. The first relates to the participation of women in military activities (they will be seen practising the wielding of arms, totally naked). The second relates to the sharing of women and children, that is to say to the

63. An Athenian is at once a citizen and a soldier. Vernant has described this Athenian homogeneity of warrior and statesman in Vernant, 1988. See more recently the indispensable book by Hanson, 2000.
64. See Brisson, 1997, pp. 95–117.

absence of domestic property among the guardians who, instead, live an entirely communal life. The third relates to the need to conflate philosophy and political power (turning philosophers into kings or kings into philosophers) in order to put an end to political troubles.[65] Socrates' emphasis and the closely argued justification of each of these three points constantly underline the risks that Socrates is taking. He could be 'torn apart', struck down on the spot by some horrified Athenian. It is true that each of these assertions calls into question the existing Athenian political and social organization. To insist that women take part in the most important of tasks is to acknowledge that they possess a status denied to them in Greek cities. To do away with family life and institute the communal sharing of women and children is to call into question the very bases of Athenian democracy, which is founded upon the division of the territory between the tribes (and their 'demes'), the division of wealth between the census classes, and the division of the domestic world between the various households (and here private ownership of the land played a particularly important role, as no attempts at reform had really tackled the inequality of the distribution of land).[66] It is harder to tell

65. It is this coincidence of political power and philosophy in a single individual that has given rise to the legendary figure of the 'philosopher-king' (a legend created by readers, for Plato himself does not use the expression). It is to be distrusted all the more both because it suggests power centred in one individual (whereas Plato uses the plural: what is needed is for 'those whom we now call our kings and rulers [to] take to the pursuit of philosophy [so that] there is a conjunction of . . . political power and philosophic intelligence', V, 473d) and because it ineptly ascribes priority to the philosopher (the expression 'king-philosopher' would do just as well). Also, if any such phrase is appropriate it must be the gender-neutral 'philosopher-ruler', since Plato explicitly allows women as well as men to constitute the guardian-class from which such rulers are drawn (*Republic*, VII, 540c).
66. Criticism of the family is a characteristic feature of Plato's political thought. I shall be returning to this subject in Chapter 5, which is devoted to the *Laws*.

whether the insistence that the kings be philosophers was regarded as the vain dream of an intellectual or as an article of faith for an oligarch who was hostile to democracy. But at any rate the contemporary Athens cannot be recognized in this picture. The city founded by Socrates (for those three measures are constitutional laws) in no way resembles Athenian democracy or its institutions, — far from it; and it is for this political reason that Socrates is afraid of being punished and arraigned.[67] Despite these difficulties and political arguments, which made precisions, diplomatic preambles and justifications necessary, the plan of the dialogue is very clear. After developing the political comparison and explaining the genesis and constitution of the city (Books II to IV) the dialogue focuses in Books V–VII on meeting the third possible wave of objections by offering a precise definition of philosophico-political competence). Finally the *Republic* describes what may become of the excellent constitution (namely, corruption) (VIII–X), before eventually responding to the very first question posed and producing a definition of a just man (end of IX).

Given that the following books merely clarify certain aspects or effects of the above, the text of Books II to IV is sufficiently autonomous to be read as one distinct part of the work, which begins with the political comparison (II, 368c) and ends with the description of the just city (IV, 444a). As Jacques Brunschwig has observed, 'the *Republic* could well end right there'; and it is true that the specificity of the enquiry and likewise of the line of argument of this preliminary investigation constitute reasons enough for us to pay it particular attention.

The genesis of the city described in Books II to IV is based upon a cumulative argument concerning the satisfaction of

67. Criticism is certainly forthcoming, although it is attenuated by all Socrates' precautions. It is of a political nature: the 'great change' introduced by Socrates is immediately described by Adeimantus as a 'complete change' to the 'political regime' (V, 449d).

needs. The reason why men come together in groups is to satisfy their basic needs, and it is also in order gradually to satisfy the needs that arise in the city that all the various professions develop. Every need creates a profession, a function. Given sufficient motivation, such a cumulative and quantitative logic is unstoppable. So Socrates imposes two limitations. First, he introduces the principle according to which functions should be exclusive (one function for each person: this is a kind of *division of labour*, II, 370b–c); secondly, he limits the proliferation of professions (II, 372f). The limit is imposed by *necessity* and is transgressed by the city when it is no longer content to satisfy fundamental and indispensable needs (food, lodging and clothing), but aspires to luxuries, that is to say to the production of new needs and the acquisition of new riches.

Book II, 370–374 presents a summary and an efficient explanation of the first part of the *Republic*. It can be reduced to a dynamic, circular schema showing how the city is affected by two contrary movements (two ways of developing): one is the movement of corruption which leads from a healthy city (II, 369) to a sick one (II, 372–374); the other is the movement of reform which purifies the city by educating the guardians (II, 374–III, 399).[68]

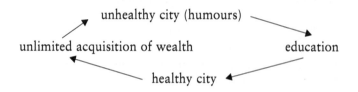

A city can thus develop in either of two kinds of opposed types of growth. One involves a pathological increase, the

68. ' "By the dog", said I, "we have all unawares purged the city which a little while ago we said was luxurious" ' (III, 399e).

principle of which is the acquisition of wealth and an accumulation of needs. The other involves education (of the guardians), the function of which is simply to limit the extension and corruption of the city. There is something strange about the idea that, if no limits are imposed, the city expands indefinitely (and thereby clashes with its neighbours).[69] This is because the unlimited acquisition of wealth is the true motor of a city's growth, and it comes to exclude all other principles. To understand this, we must distinguish, as Socrates does, between the establishment of a city and its growth. Its establishment is dictated by essential needs and it defines the city as a *cohabitation* (*sunoikia*) of human beings who, together, manage to provide for their basic needs. Its growth, on the other hand, shows that its needs, basic or otherwise, are not being satisfied. The same political preoccupation runs throughout the entire work: if a city is good, that is because it has achieved a balance, a state that cannot be modified without entailing its degradation.

Later, Books VIII and IX, in their description of political and psychological injustice, return to the message conveyed by these remarks on the pathological imbalance of the city. However, we should not conclude from this that a just city is at rest, or that Platonic politics aspire to an ideal immobility (for that would make no sense, for the simple reason that all physical things are in movement).[70] Instead, we should see from this general cycle in the health of the city that immobility may be suspended provided that the various parts of the civic community find the state of equilibrium that constitutes their common state of excellence. The most

69. It is all the more strange given that the body of the city, like that of any individual, ought to grow only within certain limits. But here, territorial expansion is not conceived as the body of the city. As we shall see, the *Republic*'s use of physiological comparisons and analogies is frequently very ambiguous.

70. But also, of course, because, provided one brings about the necessary changes (by making the power philosophical) it is possible to make the city change for the better and *become* excellent, having previously been corrupt.

important point, however, is that this condition is not a 'natural' one. The natural condition for a city is one of increasing needs and, as Socrates emphasizes, the origin (basis, *archê*) of a city 'is our needs' (II, 369c). And in so far as needs do not themselves include the principle of their own limitation and harmony, the natural way for a city to function is ever to multiply its needs. That is why it is not really a matter of accommodating or correcting this natural tendency, as Glaucon seems to want Socrates to do when he presses him to recognize that some needs are more necessary and more human than others (which are suited only to pigs, 372d). Rather, that natural tendency should be eradicated. It is necessary to impose upon the city a way of life different from its spontaneous, natural functioning, and to give it a different motivating principle. Thought must work upon the city. It is only by breaking with the natural and spontaneous form of cohabitation that politics can truly make the city a proper city (and not just a herd or fortuitously assembled gathering of human animals); and that break can only be envisaged and engineered if thought conceives of a form of gathering and a communal life that escape the cycle of needs and can be something other than a refined animal existence. The highest kind of thought (at first mathematical, then dialectical) will allow philosophers to conceive of this form of life and will enable them to govern the city so as to realize it. This great confidence in thought, which we sometimes find hard to understand or imagine because we are not accustomed to the idea of the relevance and political efficacy of philosophical thought,[71] is essentially Platonic. What the *Republic* expects from politics is not merely a measure of

71. Or we only conceive of that relevance as technical competence (thanks to our 'technocratic' ideology). The reactions of Socrates' interlocutors, and likewise the extremely hostile echo to be found in a comedy such as Aristophanes' *Clouds* (which mocks the Socratic school and all its ridiculous dreamers), suggest that Plato faced deep-seated incomprehension. However, at least the mistrust of his own day was not the indifference of today.

reflection and prudence, the kind that may be expected from any technique (a cobbler must know how a man walks and what a foot is); it demands the most perfected exercise of thought—true understanding and nothing less.

Serving the city

In the long description of Books II to IV, the city results from a piecemeal accretion of parts. But following this, when the education of the guardians makes it feasible to envisage the possibility and means of limiting that accretion and also a remedy for it, the point of departure for a second investigation is the city conceived as a whole, a unified whole. Socrates now sets out to justify or explain its hierarchical arrangement and the status of its various constitutive elements.

Once he has completed that first sketch of the city, the *Republic* is in a position to follow one of two paths as it pursues its political reflections: either the path of psychology, as adopted by the description contained in the first four books, or that of functional exercise of virtue. The former followed on from the initial comparison between state and soul; the latter, to which the dialogue now devotes itself, originated in a later argument concerning virtue.

When the *Republic* assimilates the city to the soul, it is not developing a new comparison but continuing an analysis begun in the *Gorgias*, which defined politics as the art that is concerned with the soul and its health.[72] Returning to his earlier definition of man as a soul, in the *Republic* Plato develops a psychology (or rather, here, an anthropology) which examines the various human abilities and the different kinds of behaviour that stem from a balance achievcd between three different kinds of soul. This examination is later continued in the *Phaedrus*, using similar terms: there

72. 464b–c; so politics consists of two parts, justice and legislation.

too it is a matter of explaining how the soul should be governed and how one of its 'parts' has to be sovereign if the combination of its three parts is to be balanced and just, that is to say excellent. The *Republic* thus undertakes the examination of a threefold object, the nature of which is psychological as well as political and the perfection of which, in both cases, stems from an understanding of reality (that is, of the intelligible forms). But, as was shown in the text from the *Euthydemus* cited earlier (291c4–292b3) and as is also suggested in the *Republic*, politics, which is a form of knowledge, also involves a way of using that knowledge: politics is a technique. As with all techniques, it has both a function and an object. In order to understand this better, let us now try to collect together all the remarks that the *Republic* makes about virtue and technique, two terms which, in Platonism, are inseparable.[73]

It will be remembered that, in the early dialogues, politics is treated as a matter of knowledge and virtue, the former being the cause of the latter. Whatever its field, excellence (or virtue, *aretê*) always depends upon knowledge. The *Euthydemus*, the *Meno* and the *Gorgias* all reiterate this, declaring that every reality, every object, has its own specific function, which distinguishes it from all others. And excellence is an ability to fulfil that function well. For example, one can cut a vine shoot using a knife, a chopper or some other kind of tool. But with none of these tools will the job be done as well as with a pruning knife specially designed for the task. Thus, excellence qualifies the function that this particular thing 'accomplishes better than any other'.[74] And virtue must therefore be defined as *excellence in its own particular function*. In respect of every reality, considered from the point of view of its own virtue, the question to be asked is therefore that of its function (*ergon*)

73. As I tried to point out in Pradeau, 1999, pp. 18 f.
74. *Republic*, I, 353a10–11; see 352e–353a.

[54]

and its ability (*dunamis*) to accomplish that function. This applies to the citizens of a city, each of whom will have to accomplish a single task; and it also applies to the city itself which, in its turn, with the support of justice, possesses a particular ability or potential.[75] The potential of a city always rests upon a certain form of knowledge, so the investigation of virtue links up with the investigation of the soul, and now calls for a virtuous government, that is to say a *knowledgeable* government for the city. The person or persons who govern must be capable of knowing what is suitable for each thing, so that each thing can fulfil its function in excellent fashion.

This requirement entails two consequences, and from Book V on it is these that define the role of the philosopher in the city.

In the first place he must understand each thing, in particular each group of citizens, in order to determine the nature and exercise of its function. It is this which, *from a purely political point of view*, makes knowledge of the intelligible Forms indispensable. Knowledge of the Forms is thus justified by and founded upon a political imperative. In other words, and this is certainly very important, the figure of the 'philosopher-ruler' can be regarded as the answer to a strictly political question: it is not the case that the philosopher governs because he or she is knowledgeable; rather, it is because power demands, as the condition of its *just* exercise, knowledge of *what is*, so it must produce a philosopher (in the literal sense of engendering him, since it is the city that gives birth to the philosopher)[76]. Or rather, either it gives birth to the philosopher or else it makes the ruler into a philosopher. Whichever the case may be, all that matters is that power should be appropriated by those with *knowledge*. The importance of this linkage is all the greater given that a precedent is to be found in the *Euthydemus*,

75. I, 351b f.
76. VII, 520b, which can be taken literally.

where politics is said to be sovereign not because, in itself, it possesses some kind of technical superiority, but because the distinctive feature of all techniques is that they enable or produce an overriding objective. So it is on the basis of a requirement inherent in the nature of techniques and the need to render them effective within a single city that one overriding technique has to exist, that is to say a way of putting all the city's efforts to good use.

So it is worth pointing out that political technique (or science) is not autonomous: it does not itself possess the principle of its sovereignty or power (*archê*). On the contrary, it is, rather, an outcome, the effect of a final cause, since it completes a perfection that pre-existed it (namely, the city) and constitutes a response to requirements external to it (the city must be governed wisely). Thus, according to the terms of the *Euthydemus*, the *Republic* does not consecrate politics as an absolute, self-sufficient technique. Rather, it regards it as an indispensable kind of knowledge which stems from reflection that ranges beyond the sole object of the city (just as the knowledge of a dialectician ranges beyond the field of political affairs). It is therefore impossible to confer any specific quality upon political knowledge or to accord it any technical sovereignty—unless, that is, one supposes, as do the dialogues that are later than the *Republic*, that politics actually partly *produces* its own object and itself works to set the city in order and perfect it.[77]

The next point is that the philosopher must govern. To govern excellently is to make the citizens better, virtuous and knowledgeable. That is the philosopher's function, the technique that he can adopt because he posesses sufficient understanding of reality (he is adept at dialectics, that is to say the science that understands *what is*, not just *what*

77. See further on the question of the relationship between this argument in the *Euthydemus* and the *Republic*, Kahn, 1996, pp. 208–9, Gill, 2000, especially pp. 142–43.

becomes).[78] Here then, we find the information that was lacking in the earlier dialogues: the knowledge that makes a statesman competent is dialectic, the ability to seize upon 'an account of the essence of each thing' (VII, 534b3–4).

In the *Republic*, political competence is determined finally, and teleologically, by its function. A fully developed explanation of this is to be found in Book III, where Socrates observes that the leaders of the city must be chosen from amongst the guardians (412b–415e). He explains that it is best to choose those who prove themselves, through trial and error, to be the most 'useful' to the city, the most capable of doing what is best for it. It is worth noting that this explanation is consistently governed by the logic of interest or advantage (*sumpheron*). What the city's leaders must promote is whatever is in the interest of the city as a whole. This is where their competence lies. What is remarkable and also new is that their competence does not stem from any particular faculty, let alone from one shared, to greater or lesser degree, by all people. It is simply a matter of their function (which is to govern the city in its best interest), a function that is defined, as are all techniques, by its fitness for producing its own particular object. It is this function that distinguishes the guardians from the rest of the population and it is with a view to this function, which operates as a final cause, that they are picked out and trained. It is also with a view to this function that the best of them are then selected. So it is the function of government, the function of leadership, that determines the choice of the most competent men. Plato never presupposes that all men have the ability to exercise power. Unlike some of his successors (including Aristotle) and most modern thinkers, Plato never poses the problem of *who* should govern, nor does he venture to clarify and name regimes by reference to one person who possesses and wields power. Instead, he asks

78. According to the definition given in Book VII, 533e–534b.

who is capable of assuming the function of government of which there is but one form, one kind: the right kind. Clearly, whereas the *Meno*, for example, was still wondering whether there might one day exist someone capable of governing well, the *Republic* has moved on from that position: since the person required by the function does not at present exist, he must be trained.

The political technique of the governmental function has thus, by definition, only one interest, that of the city conceived as a single entity. It is this point that one crucial text at the heart of the *Republic* seeks to establish. It is crucial because it seeks, at the level of the entire city, to verify the hypothesis that the type of government in a just city is in the interest of all the citizens. When Adeimantus complains that the lot of the guardians is an extremely hard one (denied, as they are, private property, gold and silver, and even wives and children), Socrates sets out to show him that, on the contrary, they are the happiest of all the citizens. Faced with this objection from Adeimantus, the *Republic* confronts what we may identify as the classic problem of the compatibility of private, individual interests with the interest of the city or community as a whole. How can a citizen be sure, how can he convince himself that his interests and his advantage (and likewise his happiness) depend strictly upon the interest of the city? In truth, that question is not relevant and only arises if one does not grasp the point that the interest (and happiness) of each individual is only possible, as Socrates has just explained, if the city identifies its own interest. It is, however, a crucial question since Plato does not avoid it but, on the contrary, makes use of it as a pretext to introduce an analogy that is indispensable to the definition of the city. Provoked by Adeimantus' objection, the clarification that Socrates now provides brings to an end the comparison between the soul and the city and also his description of the genesis of the city:

Our first task then, we take it, is to mould the model of a
happy state—we are not isolating a small class in it and
postulating their happiness, but that of the city as a whole.
But the opposite type of state we will consider presently.
It is as if we were colouring a statue and someone
approached and censured us, saying that we did not apply
the most beautiful pigments to the most beautiful parts of
the image, since the eyes, which are the most beautiful
part, have not been painted with purple but with black—
we should think it a reasonable justification to reply,
'Don't expect us, quaint friend, to paint the eyes so fine
that they will not be like eyes at all, nor the other parts,
but observe whether by assigning what is proper to each
we render the whole thing beautiful'. And so in the
present case you must not require us to attach to the
guardians a happiness that will make them anything but
guardians'. (IV, 420c2–e1)

This analogy (for this time it is not a comparison) enables
Socrates to dissipate any ambiguity that still remained in the
minds of his interlocutors as to the origin of the constitution
forged before their very eyes. This is not the Athenian
constitution; nor is the city whose plan the *Republic* sets
out Greek. Its material elements—the professions that it
incorporates, the institutions and even the essential fields of
its knowledge or expertise—might, like those of the *Laws*, be
described as Greek, so you could say that Plato is not
inventing his city. However, the constitutional configuration
of this material is contrary to anything known by the
Athenians and to any of their notions regarding communal
life and government. It is well attested that, along with an
admiring personification of Athens, the unity of the city
constituted a major theme for political speeches and
propaganda. But the possibility of gathering citizens together
within the single body of a city, submitting to a single
will, was generally considered conceivable only provided the
question of power was resolved by being exercised by one of

the city's 'parties' in particular.[79] The text of the *Republic* calls such an appropriation of power by one particular group an exceptional political form and, in the last analysis, a form of civil strife (a state of conflict).

It is on this account that the oligarchic ideology, according to which the 'good', or well-born, should govern the 'bad', is here condemned.[80] The traditional representation of power, that of a political regime named after the party that rules the whole city, which Aristotle was to try to pin down in his *Politics*, is alien to the thought of Plato who, once again, considers the question of the entire city back-to-front. Adopting the unity of the city as his hypothesis and point of departure, he considers the individual citizen, whoever he may be, purely as *a function of the city*. Plato's insistence upon the theme of the professions and the need for each individual to exercise a single function finds its true justification in this idea (for that of the realizability of the ideal state still remained disputable). As we have seen, the *Republic*'s three groups distinguish between three different kinds of functions: those relating to nutrition, housing, trade and services; those relating to defence; and, finally, those based on thought and government. We can now see that none of those three kinds of function is conceivable without the other two and that no citizen can live in the city without taking part in one or other of the three. So it is function that defines the city and citizenship as a form of association. A city stands for the combination and compatibility of those functions; and citizenship means exercising them.

79. Thus Pericles, while praising the unity displayed by Athens when at war, explains it by the fact that it is the people (the *dêmos*), rather than a minority, that holds power. See *History of the Peloponnesian War*, in particular the funeral oration, II, 35–46.

80. The party of the oligarchs is targeted even more explicitly in the Republic VI, 499b–500d, where Socrates explains that in the last analysis the people and the philosophers are opposed to the very same enemies, those 'few' (*oligoi*) who are hostile not only to the well-being of the city but also to knowledge.

This form of equivalence is quite different from the way in which we, in the modern age, view the relations between individuals and their community. The modern concept of a public or political system as the realization and mutual satisfaction of both the private interests of individuals and the interests of the State, or as the accidental realization of the public interest through the deliberate satisfaction of individual interests,[81] is foreign to the author of the *Republic*. That is partly for the historical reason that the Greeks were seldom inclined to allow individuals the fulfilment and autonomy that they are granted in modern times. But it is also because Plato does not consider the individual or citizen to be the primary or initial element in his thinking. On the contrary, Plato sets out to describe a process of *individuation*.

The first four books of the *Republic*, to which the passage quoted above (420c2–e1) provides a preliminary conclusion, describe the genesis of the city through the individuation of its citizens by means of a series of educational procedures and tests designed to enable each individual to recognize and accept the function that should be his in the city, in accordance with his own particular nature and abilities. To put the matter in contemporary terms, Plato does not consider the question of how a citizen can internalize the social norm that rules the city (the principal maxim of which is that 'each individual performs a function necessary for the group as a single whole'). He does not wonder how an individual adjusts his personal behaviour to this norm that consists in the well-being or interest of the community, nor how he becomes aware of and understands that norm. All that is demanded of a citizen of the *Republic* is one belief, a belief that the leaders must at all costs—even at the cost of a lie (a myth) (*Republic*, 414c–415d)—ensure that the city constitutes a single unit: an indivisible unit, obtained through

81. The first notion is paraphrased from Hegel, 1953, pp. 49–53. The second is a summary of Smith, 1976.

the institution of functions that are indispensable to its maintenance. The unity of the city is that of a plurality in equilibrium, an equilibrium that must constantly be encouraged (by producing the best possible citizens and by warding off all conditions favourable to conflict), but that will ineluctably come to suffer the process of corruption that is described in Book VIII.[82]

For the author of the *Republic*, strictly speaking, only one city exists, the one whose constitution is described in this work of his. All the cities of the past or which, far or near, still exist are cities that are corrupt and unbalanced or marked by civil strife. By definition, only one kind of city has a chance of instituting an ordered combination of functions. Just as a function is virtuous only when it excels, that is to say when it is performed in the best possible way, so too a city is virtuous only when a combination of excellent functions are brought together within a self-sufficient community. For Plato, there can only be one city of this sort: a united city. This city constitutes a community of distinct virtues, an entity composed of a combination of excellent functions, which Plato calls 'justice'. Justice is not a type of action related to a norm, nor is it any particular criterion of excellence; nor is it really a virtue. Rather, it is a sign, an indication of a combination of all the virtues. And, Plato insists, that applies both to the soul and to the city since each, being 'formed of several', needs 'to become entirely one'.[83]

---

82. It is only in Book VIII, with the catalogue of defective States and souls, that a clash, both psychological and political (according to the terms of comparison of Book II), appears between individual ends and the order of the city. In the ideal State, if anything such as a 'subjective' internalization opposed the observation of the common norm (the pattern of behaviour favourable to the unity of the city), or if any citizen set about living in contradiction to the dictates of the city, the latter would have to be failing or to have already failed.

83. See IV, 443c–e. The idea that there is really only one real city or constitution (one governed by knowledge) and that other cities are simply more or less defective versions of this one recurs also in the *Statesman* (300c–301e): see further Chapter 3 below.

What is striking about this text is that it extricates the *Republic* from the dilemma constituted by a clash between the interest of the individual and the interest of the city by pointing out that the former is merely one of the functions of the latter. That is why a citizen, or a functional group of citizens, can be said to be a potential source of power (*dunamis*) for the city. It is also why the effective exercise of those functions is always dictated by the principle of safeguarding and maintaining the equilibrium of the totality (its harmony or its health, depending on the model).[84]

In the most excellent city, as thus defined, a citizen clearly relates to his city through his function. This is his role (to exercise the function that is his), his contribution to all that is needed by the entity formed by all the citizens. However, the exercise of his function is not all there is to the life of a citizen (despite Adeimantus' apparent fears) (*Republic*, 419a). It is a mistake to consider only that aspect of the civic relationship, and to ignore the themes of the education, the culture, and the ways of life and activities which, in the *Republic*, are shared by all the citizens. The fact that mastery of the most valuable types of knowledge does not fall to the common lot but is reserved for those endowed with a natural ability, who have followed an academic programme designed to prepare them to govern the city does not mean that the rest of the citizens, with less education, are abandoned to false beliefs and random opinions. Plato is greatly concerned that opinions be correctly guided, and his concern sometimes takes the form of severe criticism of the opinions of most poets and rhetors who tend to inspire in people whose minds

---

84. In the passages just cited from the *Republic*, especially 420c2–e1, the city is compared to a living being, and that is precisely how it is personified in the early dialogues. Recourse to the vocabulary of organic functions and functional hierarchies thus becomes a particularly favoured ploy of political thought. This is all the more striking in view of the fact that elsewhere in the *Republic* the body is hardly mentioned at all.

are suggestible beliefs that are impious or contrary to the preservation of the unity of the city. His concern is that of a man who conceives of the truth not as simply a self-sufficient and autonomous realm of thought (or discourse), nor just as an (intelligible) mode of perceiving reality, but also as an inclination of the soul to desire to structure all that concerns it in accordance with such perfection as it can conceive. Thus, if you truly know what goodness or beauty is, in other words if you know the Form of the good or that of the beautiful, your soul will constantly desire and determine to encourage the presence or advent of good and beautiful things. Quite simply, it will desire to persevere in the kind of delight of which the *Phaedrus* gives the most enthusiastic account (247b–248c).

In the *Republic* truth is furthermore prolific because true knowledge of one thing is always the point of departure for the discovery of something else,[85] but also because knowledge is self-perpetuating or self-generating. Plato insists that whoever possesses knowledge should be able to teach. It is understandable, then, that in the political sphere, once he has deliberately merged the exercise of power and pedagogy (improving people), he reaches the conclusion that to govern presupposes influencing opinions, forming or encouraging them in such a way as to get them to conform with the truth. From this point of view, the principal philosophico-political objective is to produce correct opinions concerning the city and the behaviour that everyone in it should adopt. So the diversity of functions and the hierarchical separation of the functional groups do not mean that the citizens of the different groups become separate from one another as regards the objectives of knowledge and behaviour, nor that they are, as persons, irremediably set

---

85. The analogy between the Form of the good and the sun, in Book VII (507a–511d), suggests that true understanding is an ongoing process or progress.

apart.[86] To this extent the excellent Platonic city displays a social permeability and mobility very different from what an Athenian citizen could expect, integrated as he was into a taut and inflexible network of multiple loyalties relating to his family, his tribe and the census group to which he belonged.[87] In the *Republic*, citizenship involves no more than the exercise of one's function and sufficient self-control for this to be possible. In order to exercise one's function in the most excellent fashion, it is necessary to be aware that it is a function of a particular nature that is compatible and associated with all the other functions in the city. It is therefore essential that, somehow or other, every citizen regards the city as a totality, a multiple unit to which he himself belongs and which he resembles: the city is, without a doubt, an excellent *way of life*. Just as in individual life, it is important never to take the city's excellence for granted, but constantly to strive to promote it (by educating all the children and training *all* the citizens).

Political science (and politics)

Political science may be defined as the (philosophical and dialectical) understanding of what is fitting for each individual citizen and also the citizens as a whole. This is what connects the two ongoing arguments one of which concerns the soul (and is introduced by the initial comparison), while the other concerns virtue (and is introduced right at the beginning of the dialogue when Socrates asks

86. The long passage (372d–427c) devoted to the education of the guardians and the tests to which they are submitted in order to discover which of them should pursue their studies and become dialectician-leaders shows clearly enough that an individual may be ejected from one functional group and transferred to another or, on the contrary, may gain admission to another, depending on his ability to perform the indispensable function (see, in particular, II, 374b–376c and III, 412b–414b).
87. For a clear and full representation of Athenian society, see most recently Mossé, 1995.

what constitutes a just person). From then on, psychological excellence and political excellence become merged: when the governor(s) of a city is/are philosophically competent, the psychological excellence of human behaviour, the excellence of the relations between citizens, and the excellence of the city as a just entity all merge together. This is exactly what is revealed by the definition of justice as excellence in the relations between all the parts of a living whole (IV, 443a–444a). In this respect, the *Republic* certainly abandons the reticence of Socrates in the *Euthydemus* (291c–292e): now, the totality of the city's activities can be entrusted to a dialectician who possesses the *synoptic* ability necessary for excellence in all things.[88] This is a point that needs to be emphasized: it is this synoptic ability that enables the dialectician to govern. It is because he understands the 'kinship' between different kinds of teaching, that is to say their specificity, how they relate to one another and how some are subordinate to others, that the philosopher is in command of them.

However, a cognitive definition of politics (which merges political power and the knowledge of a dialectician) does not fully cover the combination of its function and its use. To define politics as a technique, a certain way of using knowledge, presupposes that it is possible to define the rules that govern it as well as its object, and the material that it moulds as well as its eventual product. As the *Euthydemus* put it, this would make it possible for us to understand how it is that politics can reign supreme over all other tech-

88. The synoptic nature of the dialogue is mentioned in Book VII, 533c–d, 534e and 537c. A dialectician is 'a man who is able to exact an account of the essence of each thing' (534b3–4) and who is capable of a synoptic view (537c6–7), which is why it is important for those (the young) naturally disposed toward philosophy 'to gather [their] studies into a comprehensive survey of their affinities with one another and with the nature of things' (537c1–7). On the relationship between the *Euthydemus* and the *Republic*, see the text to n. 77, above.

niques and all their products. For three reasons, however, the *Republic* does not fulfil that condition.

In the first place and in contrast to the *Euthydemus*, the *Republic* does not try to define the particular kind of knowledge or technique that constitutes politics; it is content simply to refer to it.[89] It never provides a definition of politics as such, but only discusses its presumed object, the city and its constitution, without defining the knowledge or art that is devoted to them.[90] And the reason why such a definition is not provided is precisely that its place is taken by the dialectic of the philosopher, as political sovereignty is merged with the science of dialectic. In the central Books of the *Republic* (V–VII), education toward knowledge of the Form of the Good is the central theme, not analysis of a specifically *political* type of knowledge. The precise way in which knowledge of the Good informs the management of the life of the city is not spelled out.

Secondly, and in consequence, the substitution of the science of dialectic for political knowledge explains how it is that the *Republic* shows hardly any interest in the way in which politics produce and use 'everything'. Such considerations, to which the *Euthydemus* seemed to attach a certain urgency, occupy no more than a marginal place in the *Republic*. The reason for this is, primarily, the nature and function of the philosopher in this most excellent of cities. He is not an artisan, nor a technician; as we have just repeated, all he does is administrate the perfection that has been achieved: that is the educational nature of his political function. In the *Republic*, Plato draws a distinction between

89. Only once does the *Republic* mention the existence of a 'political technique', associating it, through an example, with painting and music: VI, 493d3. It never uses the expression 'political science'. The rarity of those terms should therefore caution prudence, if not invite astonishment: the *Republic* does not have much to say about politics. Contrast *Euthydemus*, 291c–292e.
90. The objects of politics, or its domain, are 'city affairs', *politika*; see in particular III, 407d4; VI, 496c3 and 498b8; VIII, 558b7; IX, 592a5.

the philosopher-ruler and another kind of political technician, namely the city's *founders*, that is to say Socrates and
his interlocutors. Rather than the philosopher who, for his
part, governs the city, it is they who, 'in their discourse'
found the city (II, 369a). In Book VII, 519c8,[91] Socrates
again describes them as the 'founders' of the city, founders
whose function is to ensure that their creation is governed by
philosophers.[92] The creation they have fashioned, the city, is
presented in its entirety as a picture, a canvas upon which
the founders draw a plan, in imitation of the divine model
(VI, 500d–501c). This important technical comparison (a
city-founder is a kind of artisan) can only be understood if
one draws a clear distinction between the roles that it
attributes to each of the different characters involved. The
'designer of political constitutions' is not the governor of the
city; he simply sketches the plan, the blueprint (501a9–c6),
imitating a divine and ordered model which, on the last page
of Book IX, is said to be possibly 'up in heaven' (592b).[93]
The picture is thus a copy, which creates human characters
'in the image and likeness of God' (VI, 501b). The one
who governs the city has played no part in the design of
these characters. His role is simply to distribute them in
accordance with their nature.

The third and last reason for the *Republic*'s silence about
the specifics of political practice and the political art is

91. *Hoi oikistai* are those who set up or install a dwelling place. The term
covers both founders and colonizers. (In the *Laws*, the Athenian uses it to
refer to Clinias and the 'nine other founders' of the colony, V, 753a9).

92. 'It is the duty of us, the founders, . . . to compel the best natures', VII,
519c. And that constraint is applied in the name of the perfection of the
whole city.

93. The 'divine model' to which the text alludes is that of the stars, the
movement and disposition of which are perfect, in so far as movements can
be. Plato, rejecting the Athenian religion (that of the Olympian gods, whose
actions and passions he considers to be too human), consecrates as divine
the living beings whose (corporeal and psychological) perfection is the
greatest: namely the stars. The gods are, first and foremost, the planets and
the stars.

the interlocutors' lack of interest in the nature and the organization of physical bodies in the city. It would be possible to establish this simply by pointing to the fact that the analogue of the city with its three classes is the soul with its three kinds, and then to argue that this psychological comparison obliges the discussion to confine itself to the domain of thought and characters (for the individual characters of Book VIII in effect reproduce the condition of the city). But a more precise critique seems to be called for.[94] The *Republic* provides no description of human bodies nor, more generally, of 'human and mortal things' (nor does it make any mention of geography or of architecture, for all such objects have been dismissed along with the luxury of the fevered city) (*Republic*, II, 372e–373a). This can be explained in two ways. First, by pointing out that the *Republic* represents the city as an imitation of a psychological, or even divine, model, and that it can therefore be content to appeal to relatively vague forms of organization or harmony that are devoid of any physical dimension. But it can also be explained by showing that, by omitting to give politics any particular technical or epistemological status, the *Republic* gives it no specific object. Indeed, by making the philosopher the ruler, it prevents politics from becoming the subject of any form of activity other than that of making laws. The governor has no particular object, but he legislates in such a way that, among the objects that exist, some are controlled or excluded. The best proof of this is provided by the 'diseased' expansion of the city in Book II (*Republic*, 373b–e). The *Republic* never returns to the healthy constitution that Socrates imagines initially (a constitution that only addresses indispensable needs; 369a–372d). On the contrary, surprisingly enough, the point of departure for an excellent constitution is the sick city, a city that harbours

---

94. It is a criticism of his presentation in the *Republic* that Socrates himself will make at the beginning of the *Timaeus* (19b–c). See below, the beginning of IV, 2.

a multitude of professions and guardians (for, having trespassed on neighbouring territories, the city is obliged to go to war). Thus, at the end of Book IV, perfection is achieved at the price of defining the functions of each individual together with a legal constraint the purpose of which is to arrange the various classes so that they relate to one another, by attributing to each one a particular quality and function.[95] Before achieving perfection, the city has had to be corrected and purged. Politics thus consists simply in a philosophical purging of pre-existing material, and that is why it is not a specific technique.

The *Republic* is an unprecedented and provisional constitution. Plato measures it against a well-established genre of political literature, that of the prose treatise devoted to studying political constitutions and defining the best kind of city.[96] However, he modifies the principal basis upon which such a treatise rests. Contrary to the existing, partisan character of such treatises, which compete against one another to get power passed to the person or people whose party they serve, Plato sets out to represent whoever governs as the ultimate outcome of the way that the various elements that make up the city are organized and the mode of exercising power that goes with that organization. In other words, depending on whether the city is excellent or merely oligarchic, or even democratic, the person or persons who govern are more or less knowledgeable and, likewise, the citizens are more or less good. The governors and the governed, and the disposition of their souls thus become the results and indicators of the value of the constitutions described. This is made particularly clear in Book VIII, in which, as he lists each regime, Plato suggests a corresponding

95. This is the crucial point. The *Republic* sees legislation purely as a correcting constraint. As I shall show in due course (in Chapter 5), the last dialogues, in contrast, define the law as a kind of *constitutive* limitation of the city.

96. On the genre of constitutions, see Jacoby, 1949, and Bordes, 1982.

individual and a mode of understanding that it fosters. The philosopher makes his examination of the city the point of departure for political reflection, and makes its unity the ultimate aim of political thought and action. His concept of political science is thus quite simply a dialectic that is applied to further the interest of the city: what needs to be done is to seize upon the reason why the city is as it is. What is elaborated and described in the *Republic* is never rejected in the later dialogues, which continue to regard the administration of the city as an education, ruled by knowledge and designed to safeguard the city against a corruption that is, however, inevitable. On the other hand, the ideas of the unity of the city and of its interest undergo a series of modifications designed to remove the ambiguities, if not the limitations, of the psychological and educational model adopted by the *Republic*. As Socrates points out, the latter is, after all, no more than a plan or sketch.

3

Producing the city: the Statesman

In treating politics as a technique, Plato recognizes the
obligation of defining its material and specifying how this is
used. What does politics use and what does it take care of?
How does it operate? What is the nature of its material and
who can make use of it? By now we know the answers to
these questions and they are invariable, albeit at a general
level: the material of politics is the city as a whole and
the technician who shapes it is a knowledgeable governor,
a philosopher. The task of supplementing these general
answers with a precise account of the technical functioning
of the political art falls to the *Statesman*. In this dialogue,
Plato describes the technique of the political craftsman who
governs the city by comparing it to another technique
that operates in a similar fashion: namely, weaving. The
'statesman' who produces the unity of the city by getting its
diverse and in some cases opposed elements to live together
there produces a woven tissue.

The conditions necessary for political technique

To understand the political enquiry of the *Statesman*, we
must rely on the *Republic*, which constitutes its doctrinal
basis. It is within the framework defined by the *Republic*
that the *Statesman* endeavours to resolve certain difficulties
and to clarify certain points. In the *Republic*, Socrates' three

principal interlocutors are Thrasymachus, Glaucon and Adeimantus who, each in turn and with considerable virulence, criticize a serious defect in Socrates' argument. They thus afford him an opportunity to justify his arguments or to set them out differently. The three objections, which all arise out of different discussions, turn out to be one and the same when considered from the point of view of interest. Thrasymachus' objection relates directly to this subject: it is inconceivable that, as Socrates has claimed, the governors rule with a view to the interest of those whom they govern.[97] Later on, Glaucon jeers at Socrates' healthy city, calling it a city of pigs from which all truly human refinements are excluded. Finally, at the end of Socrates' description of the life led by the guardians, Adeimantus takes over (419a), accusing Socrates of giving his guardians a wretched life. As can be seen, it is the same objection that is in each instance repeated, for each time what is criticized is the way in which Socrates flouts the personal interest first of the citizens as a whole, then of the guardians in particular.

To this repeated objection, which assumes that what is in the interest of an individual is whatever gives him most pleasure, Socrates, in the *Republic*, offers one and the same reply: all individual interests must be subordinated, as secondary consequences, to securing the interest of the whole (which constitutes its unity). He does so first in answer

97. See the discussion in Book I, 341d–342d, where Socrates explains that whatever the art under consideration may be, it procures or produces a certain advantage, an 'interest' (*sumpheron*). He clarifies this definition of a technique by going on to explain that this interest is never that of the technique itself, nor that of the technician, but always that of the object. Thus, the interest of medicine is that of the body (health), not that of medicine itself nor that of the doctor. Determining the interest of the object is therefore not only a pre-requisite of any technical prowess, but also its end purpose, for it is with a view to the interest of the object that the technique is employed (medicine is exercised with a view to health). If there is such a thing as a political technique, a governmental technique, its only end purpose can be the interest of those governed.

to Thrasymachus, explaining that the one who leads and governs understands and tends the interest (or health) of whoever is subject to him; next, in answer to Glaucon, explaining that personal needs must be satisfied in proportion to the satisfaction of all; and finally, in answer to Adeimantus, showing that the interest of the city as a whole is the sole condition, the sole cause of the interest of each of its parts.

The only interest in the city is thus that of the city as a whole; the interest of the city constitutes its unity. However, although Socrates' response is as consistent as it is simple, it nevertheless remains very vague and altogether disconcerting when set alongside the definition of a technique in terms of interest. It is vague to the extent that Socrates never directly refutes the presuppositions of his interlocutors and merely substitutes a real interest (the city as a whole) for what he reckons to be a false interest (the satisfaction of personal pleasures), being content in this way to set in opposition two apparently heterogeneous objects.[98] Furthermore, in Book I, Socrates' reply only refers to the specific interest of each technique, and does not really show how, from a technical point of view, it is possible for the interest of 'all' (if not the 'general' interest) to override all the particular technical activities put together. Nor does it explain how each of the techniques can play its part and participate in the elaboration and care of this political totality that is the city. To the third of the above-cited objections, Socrates produced a response that depended upon well-being. The question that then arose was how the particular interests that distinguish the various techniques can contribute to the common well-being. Very clearly, caring for the whole of the city is the specific object of the governor, so one can see that the 'philosopher-ruler' is responsible for directing activities in

98. Instead of explaining, for example, how the unity of the city will enable every individual to satisfy his desires better than in any other situation, or that his health and well-being will be maximized.

the city in such a way that they serve the common well-being. But, again, the *Republic* does not explain how technical processes are associated with, and directed toward, this end.

The question of interest nevertheless paves the way for an enquiry that is continued in the later dialogues. If a technique takes care of and governs its object, and if the interest of its object is the function that defines it, the reason for this is that this object is to some extent defective (just as medicine exists because bodies fall sick). The cause of the technique is the defectiveness of its object, and its function consists in furthering the latter's interest. This is a rather surprising idea given that this interest is neither a judgement nor a deliberate end decided by a subject (seeking its 'interest' or 'advantage'); rather, it is a *condition*, the condition of the object that best suits its nature. To procure the interest of a living being who is sick is to restore his health; to procure that of a weaver is to provide him with ready-carded wool. But how does one determine the relation that exists between the nature of the object and its interest? In the *Republic*, Socrates provides no more than an allusive answer to this question, one that takes the form of an analogy with the effect of other arts: to a sick body medicine gives health; to a sailor the pilot gives security. In this form, the logic governing the technical definition of interest differs in no way from that which serves to define the mutual satisfaction of needs in a healthy city. The association of people makes it possible for each one to obtain satisfaction for his own particular numerous needs (II, 369b–d); in this way each individual obtains what he lacks. This is a quantitative logic. It is the distinction and addition of individual functions, with each person serving a single function, that makes it possible to satisfy the needs of all of them. It is also, as the genesis of the city shows, an associative logic, since those needs can only be satisfied if all those functions are fulfilled simultaneously. The difficulty (or defect) that the city sets out to remedy lies in combining elements that are distinct and insufficient (lacking self-sufficiency). As we have seen, the *Republic* does not provide a technical description of this relationship between interests and needs. The relations between citizens and between their needs and their interests are, instead, defined in psychological terms, on the model of the three types of soul. Or, to be more precise, it is justice that somehow takes over the resolution of the problems connected with relations between the various elements of the city. Justice is introduced immediately after the comparison in Book II:

> 'Where then, can justice and injustice be found in it [the State, or city]? And along with which of the constituents that we have considered does it come into the State?' 'I cannot conceive, Socrates', he said, 'unless it be in some need (*khreia*)[99] that those very constituents have of one another'. 'Perhaps that is a good suggestion', said I. (II, 371e11–372a4).

This ethical and political criterion for justice makes it possible, following this discussion, to identify a qualitative yardstick that is indispensable for setting limits to the quantitative multiplication of needs and technical products. But, in consequence, the relative arrangement of techniques and their relations, in particular regarding their hierarchical status, comes to be neglected. The well-being and likewise the coherence of the city as a whole are to be founded upon justice, understood as meaning everyone's realization of his own particular function.

Yet, even in the *Republic*, there was a possible way of reconciling the two points of view inherent in any technical process (that of its competence in relation to its use and that of its organization in accordance with its interest) in such a way as to conceive how to organize the techniques in relation to one another and, above all, to explain how some

99. *Khreia*, which also means use, how a thing is employed.

norm, a qualitative measure, could determine that arrangement. This arrangement, in its turn, affects the relations that bind people and their activities together, principally, however, from the point of view of their utility, the way they are put to use (*khrêsis*). In the *Statesman*, the investigation into the specific technical nature of the government of a city is carried forward on two fronts. The Stranger who leads the discussion develops the comparison between weaving and politics in order to arrive at a definition of the technique of government, and at the same time attempts to establish how to discriminate between politics and all the other techniques which, given that they resemble it, might take its place.

It is worth remembering that, in general, the *Statesman* claims to pursue an enquiry begun in the *Theaetetus* and continued in the *Sophist*, the object of which is to propose definitions of a sophist, a statesman and a philosopher. The *Statesman* is thus committed to defining a statesman. Many glosses have been produced on the unfinished nature of this enquiry, to explain what has happened to the definition of the third figure, the philosopher. But to me that question and the speculations to which it continues to give rise seem to constitute a false problem that is resolved well enough by reading the *Sophist* and the *Statesman*, and for two reasons. In the first place, if you think about what the *Sophist* says of the eponymous character whom it portrays as the epitome of falsity, you can see that this dialogue is really proposing a definition of true knowledge, of a kind that can be called philosophical. Similarly, politics, as defined in the *Statesman*, presupposes the existence of a knowledge and an activity which, as the *Republic* suggests, is clearly possessed only by a philosopher. The philosopher and philosophy are thus, by contrast, presented in the *Sophist* and in the *Statesman* both as the main alternative to sophistry and as indispensable for the kind of thought and political activity that befits the nature of the city. Secondly, the enquiry in these two dialogues is conducted in such a way that it not only provides a definition of those two eponymous figures, the sophist and the statesman, but furthermore represents dialectical discourse. In this sense, the mode of the enquiry is philosophical: to define a sophist and a statesman is, in itself, to demonstrate how philosophy should proceed. So it would be altogether absurd to conclude that the philosopher is neglected, for it is he who is the real subject of both enquiries, together with the understanding and method that define his specific kind of knowledge.

However, we still need to assess the overall project. We need to understand how it is that these three figures are linked and why they all need to be defined in relation to each other. Here again, it seems to me that it is the status of philosophy that is at stake. One might quite simply argue that sophistry and politics are both (and in equal measure) activities and kinds of knowledge to which philosophy, itself a kind of knowledge and a way of life, is linked. It either seeks to distance itself, as in the case of sophistry (from the earliest dialogues), in order to defend a new kind of knowledge, or else it attempts to refound or even appropriate it, as in the case of politics (at least from the *Euthydemus*, the *Apology* and, of course, the *Republic* onward). It is thus precisely for reasons pertaining to the institution (in every sense of the term) of philosophy that this twofold enquiry is essential. This is just as essential, at least as regards its purpose, as the enquiry that prompted the *Republic* (the aim of which, already, was to establish philosophy as true knowledge of what is *and also* to merge it with the government of the city). Of course, the epistemic and political basis of philosophy which the *Statesman* helps to establish is not quite the same, as regards either its organization or its means, as that proposed by the *Republic*. But the underlying principles and requirements are the same: one must be a dialectician in order to define and master political competence.

However, if the dialogues are distinguishable (which does not necessarily mean that we have to speculate about their relative chronology), we must be able to specify the subject to which the *Statesman* is devoted, as compared to other dialogues that also discuss the statesman, his knowledge and his technique, or the city. When we compare the *Statesman* with the *Republic*, we realize that the particular feature of the *Statesman* is that it conducts an unprecedented critical and analytical study, which involves an operation of selection. It operates at two levels, which help us to see that political enquiry and dialectical exchange are inseparable. In order to define the statesman and his political role, it is necessary to distinguish him from his aides (those who assist him in his work) and his rivals (those who seek to take his place). So it is not possible to bring the political enquiry to a satisfactory conclusion without possessing and using the necessary philosophical tools. These are by no means limited to the method of division, for in this dialogue Plato seems to employ all the principal means at the disposal of a philosopher in the conduct of an enquiry:

1. the analysis of stories (including a specifically philosophical 'mythology')[100];
2. the use of division;
3. the use of the paradigm.

From this, we can see that, as it seeks to define the *politikos* (statesman), philosophy at the same time proves or demonstrates its own ability to define an object and to pronounce upon the suitable resolution of a problem or a matter of public interest. In other words, philosophy not only demonstrates its own knowledge and methodological skill, but also—and above all—proves its ability to define what is best for human affairs, for self-government and for the government of others in the city. This was, in fact, the project undertaken by philosophy already in the *Republic*. If we concentrate on the main arguments of that dialogue, we see that the *Statesman* remains faithful to the messages of the

100. On this, see Brisson, 1998a.

Republic, including the main one: that only a knowledge-able government of the city has the power to produce the excellence (*aretê*) of which it is capable. But the demonstration of this thesis proceeds along different paths and confronts questions and difficulties that the *Republic* did not encounter. The *Republic* argued that the city would achieve excellence once it, like the soul of an individual, managed to get each of its powers or parts to accomplish its own particular function and attain to the excellence that befitted it. At that point, the city as a whole (like the soul as a whole) could achieve the excellence constituted by justice. According to the *Republic*, this meant that it was necessary to distinguish between the various parts or powers of the whole, in order to establish between them the hierarchy that would befit their best possible government. The *Statesman* pursues the very same aim. The objective to which it is directed is, as is worth repeating, the very same as that of Platonic thought generally: namely, to allow the city to attain to the excellence constituted by its unity. However, the means described for achieving that objective differ from one dialogue to another and the shift from one paradigm to another (from an individual soul to a woven tissue) alters the way that that objective is conceived. Thus, the two points that seem to distinguish the *Statesman* from the *Republic* are the following:

1. the revision of the status and political role of virtues or character,[101]
2. a new line of thought on political competence, which is now conceived as a technique.

Producing the unity of the city is now a matter of a technical operation of a particular kind, a *technê politikê*.

---

101. I shall return to this point at the end of this chapter, p. 99 f.

The object of politics

The usefulness of a piece of work lies in its ability to carry out the use for which it is designed. This is explained in the *Cratylus* at 388b–390d,[102] where Plato shows, in particular, that the correct way of using an instrument (using it 'as one should', as Socrates puts it) is precisely what makes it possible to harmonize the two essential terms in any technical process. The cognitive competence of the technician (who understands the form of the object (its *eidos*, 389b3), merges with the object's best interest once the craftsman has discovered the instrument which, by its nature, is appropriate to each object (389b3). Usage is thus not solely an instrumental category; it is above all the particular effect of an 'eidetic' understanding (understanding in accordance with the intelligible Form, the *eidos*).[103] It is an understanding the particular feature of which is that it is recognized by the person using the instrument. The one 'who is likely to know whether the proper form of shuttle is embedded in any piece of wood' will not be 'the carpenter' but 'the weaver, who is to use it' (390b1–3). These remarks in the *Cratylus* clarify two points in the argument of the *Republic* from which they derive. In the first place, they distinguish two kinds of understanding: that of the technician (understanding of the form enables him to choose the appropriate instrument), and that of the user (who understands what is in the interest of its object).[104] Secondly—and this explains the previous distinction—usage makes it possible to subordinate the organization (or, so to speak, the government) of such works to the realization of interest:

102. This analysis is similar to that in Book I of the *Republic*, (332c–333e and 338c–347e) but is fuller and more detailed.
103. The producer does not need to know the intelligible Form from which the object he is making stems; a correct opinion of the object and its use is enough.
104. Only the user can claim that knowledge with certainty, that is to say only he can recognize whether the craftsman has given a suitable form to his material (390b).

technical products are subject to the rule of those who use them. The one who uses the object (a lyre player, say) must direct the work of the one who produces it (the lyre maker). That is why the former must convey to the latter an appropriate understanding, sufficient for him to make the artefact that he produces meet the demands of the user. This is also why the producer's specific kind of understanding consists in an ability to discover what instrument is best able to serve its purpose.

The effect of these clarifications is to draw a distinction between two kinds of technique: the techniques of production, those necessary for working on the object, or manufacturing it, and the techniques of using it, for making use of the object that is produced. Consider, once again, the example of the lyre maker and the lyre player. Each of their two respective techniques presupposes and implements a particular eidetic understanding, and the various techniques employed can be arranged in a hierarchical order, with the technique of the producer always ruled by and subordinate to the technique of the user.

In the *Euthydemus*, Plato insisted that all the other techniques 'handed over the management of the productions of their own trades' to the royal technique of politics, for 'this one alone knew how to use them' (291c7–8). Within the ordered collection of techniques, in which these are distinguished according to the use that governs them, politics, if it is to be the truly sovereign technique, must therefore govern all the uses to which the techniques are put. The text from the *Euthydemus*, cited above, made this claim, but said nothing about how the products of techniques could be made subordinate to, and thus serve, the use for which those products are destined.[105] As we have seen, technically speaking this is,

---

105. The question that arises concerns the technique (of production) that politics uses. Does it make use of all the techniques for all kinds of productions, or of a single technique the product of which is immediately at the disposal of politics? The *Statesman* favours the first of those two hypotheses.

in the first instance, because the *Republic* does not define politics as a technique. A close reading of the more specific claims of the *Cratylus* and the hypotheses of the *Euthydemus* alerts us to the fact that the *Republic* does not use the distinction between production and usage in order to define political competence and activity. This is, quite simply, because it considers politics to be a philosophical kind of knowledge that is quite different from the productions of craftsmen, and quite distinct from the other functions and activities carried on in the city.[106] This is why the exercise of power takes on the aspect of an educational framework or of legislation (that either authorizes or bans certain activities), but is never seen as a product. It would be fair to say of the *Republic* that it envisages politics solely from the point of view of how it is used: the philosopher-ruler reigns over a city whose citizens he renders knowledgeable and virtuous by forcing each one of them to perform nothing but his own particular function. So, to educate these citizens who are truly the objects of his political knowledge, he can hardly intervene in any way except as an educator. In a sense—and this is the difficulty that the *Statesman* has to resolve—it is the very doctrine of the philosopher-ruler that is threatened until it actually comes about that philosophy is given technical sovereignty.

The *Statesman* begins with a myth, the message of which is the following: politics came into existence at the moment when human beings, abandoned by the gods and forced to look after their own lives, had to master the techniques essential for their survival (273e–275a). Such mastery was a communal affair and, like the mutual satisfaction of needs in the *Republic*, it presupposed a city. If philosophy is to preserve its status (on the basis of the hypothesis according

---

106. From a cognitive point of view, this heterogeneity is precisely that of the opinion held (at best) by the citizens, whereas knowledge of *what is* remains the distinctive attribute of philosophers.

to which that mastery will only be real if it is at the same time the most elevated kind of knowledge), philosophy must, in its turn, be defined as a technique: philosophy is the best at politics. To put that more clearly: politics is a technique and the person who is best at politics is the one we call 'a philosopher'.

The distinction between techniques of production and techniques of usage plays no specifically political role up until the *Statesman*.[107] The latter, responding to the hope expressed in the *Euthydemus*, upsets the schema of the *Republic*'s political doctrine in several respects. The *Statesman* is the first Platonic text, and also the first philosophical text, ever to treat politics wholly as a technique. According to this view, endowed with a specific understanding of his object, the political technician fashions his material and designates it for a particular use.

The first consequence of politics being thus defined as a technique in this way is that, with political power and the objects it governs no longer confined to the educational and law-giving framework to which the *Republic* consigned them, their scope is considerably extended. Once it is conceived as a technique, politics is no longer defined simply as a philosophical skill, but as the ultimate and most important cog in the machine of production and usage that combines all the technical activities in the city to form a single whole. So either in a direct or a mediated fashion, politics now affects all the works that are produced in the city and the scope of its effects extends to the city's very limits. Even before undertaking a detailed study of the constitutional modifications that may distinguish the *Republic* from the *Statesman*, it is important to note that the latter dialogue sets out to give politics both an object and a

107. See Cambiano, 1991, pp. 200–4.

function,[108] which are distinct from those of the art of questioning (dialectic) and also from all other techniques. Politics has an object, furthermore, rather than a subject;[109] and a function that is not just a way of using that object but that now becomes a product. In this way, the *Statesman* reunites products and the way they are used, just as the *Euthydemus* required. In fact, it carries this to the point of defining politics precisely as the only technique (the only science) capable of merging the use and the production of its object: politics both produces the city and also governs it.

Here is a detailed plan of the dialogue:

257a1–258b2: Prologue: the object of the discussion and the choice of its interlocutors
258b2–268d4: the first definition of politics
 258d–258e7: division of the sciences into those that are practical and those that are theoretical
 258e8–259d6: the royal science as a single unit
 259d7–268d4: the division of theoretical science
  262a5–263b12: on the method of division: genus, species and part
  266d11–267a3: the shortest way to define the king
  267a4–267c4: summary and result of that division
  267c5–268d4: the defect of the division; the problem of rivals
268d5–277c8: the new way–myth

108. Those modifications are less considerable than has often been suggested. From the *Republic* right down to the *Laws*, Plato preserves the same ideal: government of the city by knowledgeable and virtuous citizens. On the consistency of this ideal and its implications for the nature of the best type of regime (which is aristocratic in the sense that only the best citizens are those that know), see Lane, 1995, pp. 276–91.
109. The 'disappearance' of the subject of politics is one of the consequences of the line taken by the enquiry in the *Statesman*, which, starting from the question of the statesman (after discussing the sophist), ends up by defining politics as an art (without explicitly defining the nature of the person who engages in it).

268d5–274e3: the myth

274c4–275c8: the message of the myth and a correction to the division

277a3–277c8: the difficulty

  277d1–305e1: the paradigm

  277d1–278e3: definition of the paradigm

  278e4–283a9: weaving as a paradigm for the technique of politics

    (281d7–281e6: productive techniques and auxiliary techniques)

  283a10–287b1: interlude—the just measure and dialectics

  287b1–305e1: application of the paradigm

    287b4–289c3: introduction: the seven kinds of objects used

    289c4–303d3: separating the rivals

    (291c8–303b7: constitutions)

    303d4–305e1: separating the auxiliaries

305e2–311c8: definition of the political technique

  306a8–308b9: the conflict between the parts of virtue

  308b10–311c9: political science as a synthetic science

As he applies the paradigm of weaving to politics, asking himself what is the material upon which politics has to work, the Stranger enumerates the various kinds of objects that constitute 'the things people possess in a city' (287e1–2). There are seven kinds and they are sufficiently distinct to cover all the objects that might exist in the city (these include instruments, containers, vehicles, shelters, amusements, materials and nutritive resources).[110] This constitutes a *political system of objects*, which complements the typology of productions and enables the Stranger to set the statesman once and for all apart from his auxiliaries and rivals, whom he restricts to making use of some object belonging to one of the seven different kinds.

The use of the term 'system' at this point may seem

110. 287d–289c.

surprising. But it is appropriate to the project, at once methodological and political, of reuniting in a single whole (*sustêma*) all the objects that make up the city. Far from taking a step backwards in a pragmatic return to the 'real' constraints which might appear to be the necessary alternative to the Utopian idealism of the *Republic*, the *Statesman* sets out to extend the field of politics to include all the city's objects, that is to say all its human affairs. From an epistemological point of view, the aspiration of political science is thus considerably greater than it was in the earlier dialogues. Deciding, as it does, upon all activities by ruling upon the use to which they are put, politics becomes the science of how to use all things. It is certainly dialectic, in the sense that an understanding of how to use things is, in the last analysis, an understanding of the Forms, but it also involves an understanding of all the practices and techniques subordinated to it. That is why it is important to make no mistake about its nature and to distinguish it clearly from all other ('rival') techniques that might try to take its place (and reduce politics to, for instance, rhetoric or military power, or a court of justice, as the case might be).

So what kind of knowledge is needed for exercising the political technique? It must be a kind of knowledge that concerns the particular kind of totality that a city is: a knowledge that understands, if not *all* objects, at least the use to which the city's citizens can and should put them; a knowledge, finally, capable of organizing all the objects thus set in order in such a way as to achieve their purpose. Political knowledge will therefore not be the sum of other individual kinds of knowledge, but rather an understanding of how the latter should be used. We should fully understand that to govern does not mean directing or quantifying what is produced but, even prior to that, deciding on how products should be used. In other words, the purpose of the political system expounded here is not to be a system of different types of knowledge. The sole ambition of politics as a science is to organize objects and different kinds of

[87]

knowledge with a view to a single end. It therefore derives its hegemony from its ability to establish intermediaries and relations between the objects that it brings together, and to limit those objects (in exactly the same way as a population or a territory must be quantitatively limited in order to promote the coherence and permanence of the city). This definition can only be justified by subsequently setting out a similar system for producing essentially political inter-relations and intermediaries (such as marriages, opinions and laws). At this point, however, all that needs to be emphasized is that the objects enumerated and classified in the *Statesman* are what constitute the city: all of them, ranging from instruments to domestic animals, are in its possession, that is to say, are parts of it. The city is con-stituted by this system of objects that are used by the citizens, all of whom need to exercise one of the techniques relating to the production or acquisition of these objects. In this way, all the techniques become indispensable since they answer the needs that individuals acquire in accordance with the city's need for unity.

This is exactly the same concern as that expressed in the *Republic*, but here its definition is given a zoological slant, in a sense indicated by the beginning of *Republic* Book IV (where the city is called a living being or animal, a *zôon*). The *Statesman* thus takes over what the *Republic* intimated but only by analogy: the city is a collection, a unit created by a heterogeneous multiplicity, which exists simply in order to hold those multiple elements together and to allow them to live in a uniform way. The unity of the city, which is the constant purpose of the system, gives politics its function: in that it is designed to ensure the government of living beings, politics is the technique of ways to live.

This new definition of the city enables Plato to resolve the difficulty that was connected with the genesis and growth of the city in the *Republic*. There the addition of new needs and professions, and the indefinite growth of the city, could only be halted by the imposition of external limitations: either by war, which was inevitable when a territory never stopped expanding; or else by the creator of the city himself, who would condemn its moral corruption and attack its luxuries. In the *Statesman*, the teleological or final cause represented by the city's unity replaces the mechanical cause of the multiplication of professions so as to determine the exact number and nature of the techniques needed.

That definition also makes it possible for Plato no longer to discuss the realization of the city in a genetic fashion, part by part, condition after condition, but instead to envisage it as a creation which, right from the start, has all its material at its disposal. That was already the case in Book IV of the *Republic* but, unlike the *Republic*, here the city is to be realized not only because it is ruled by one of its better parts (the knowledgeable guardians), but also because of the whole body of the statesman's subordinates, that is to say all the servants evoked by the Stranger, who range all the way from slaves to sophists.[111] The political effect of the presence of these classes of auxiliaries is that the city may now be considered as a specific collection of objects and living beings, all of them identified according to their respective uses or functions. So, discussing the city will necessarily entail discussing all the objects that are used by the citizens in carrying out their functions. As far as political doctrine is concerned, that is the consequence of the definition of the political art, and it is a consequence the effect of which will be all the greater because it will oblige that doctrine to take account of and combine all the various kinds of knowledge relating to products and the use to which they are put.

From the purely technical point of view, therefore, the criterion of usage does govern the arrangement and

111. 289c–291c; the shopkeepers, wage-earning workers, magistrates' assistants, diviners and priests. So it cannot be said that the 'philosopher-king' disappears from the *Statesman*; rather, the function that was his is now described taking account of the other functions from which it is inseparable.

subordination of objects and products in a satisfactory manner. But, although it makes it possible to set up a seamless hierarchy of skills, it still does not attribute to the political art any particular product or use, or even an object.

Political demiurgy

In accordance with the analogy of weaving, which is its paradigm, politics ought to produce an object, some kind of tissue. But, as has frequently been pointed out, politics, strictly speaking, produces nothing. The Stranger defines politics as a science 'of command' and says that politics is 'epitactic', directed toward action (292b9–10). Action is its end purpose, but it is itself allotted no practical task (305d1–2). As Monique Dixsaut has explained with clarity, the function of the royal science is 'not to allow any practice to free itself from political authority', by deciding for itself on the opportunity (*kairos*) that it offers.[112] The Statesman thus exercises a theoretical (not physical, 259c and 305d) power over practical skills (all the techniques that are subordinated to it) by deciding to use them and to bring them into play when he judges this to be necessary. And this is what makes politics, *par excellence*, the ultimate technique of how to use things. This, says the Stranger, is why 'embracing its capacity with the appellation belonging to the whole, we would, it seems, most appropriately call [this] statesmanship' (305e4–6). 'Belonging to the whole' here refers to the city's activities as a whole but, at the same time, also to the whole collection of objects of which the city makes use. Politics determines the use to which a totality, namely the city, is put. But does that mean that it produces nothing within that totality? And should we deduce from its epitactic nature, which aims at action but remains inactive, that it is incapable of being 'demiurgic' or 'poietic'?

The final pages of the *Statesman* define politics from the

112. Dixsaut, 1995.

point of view of its paradigm, weaving, as an intermeshing of opposed features (308b–311c). Thus defined, politics *does* produce some kind of work or product. This productive function of politics is worth examining in detail. The *Statesman* provides a very clear description of it, the principal terms of which are set out below, together with an identification of the function performed in each case by the statesman, the material that he uses and, finally, the product that results.

- Generally, he 'puts together' disparate elements so as to 'fabricate' a product. To that end, he makes use of their respective characters (*êthê*) and from them produces 'some simple kind of thing with a simple capacity' (308c–d).
- He does not work on his own, but 'presides' over the efforts of his auxiliaries, using a 'mixture' of them.[113] By working on educated characters, he produces characters of a kind to foster the virtues of 'courage and self-restraint' (308e–309b).
- He 'links', 'interconnects' and 'assembles' his material. Only a statesman has the ability to 'produce' an opinion in those who have been correctly educated. So he makes the most of such linking, using a mixture of energetic characteristics and moderate characteristics, so as to produce temperate, wise and just dispositions (309b–e).
- He 'conceives of' and 'realizes' links between the gods and human beings, using as his material honest opinions and marriages, and getting the different parts of virtue to unite (310a–b).
- Finally, his activity is to produce a fabric, using concord and friendship to realize a tissue that envelops every part of the city, producing ' a happy state [city]' (311b–c).

---

113. *sunkrasis*, and then *summixis*, at 308e8 and 309b2. This is worth noting, as in the *Timaeus* these functions will become those of the demiurge. Brisson has made an exhaustive study of this in 1998b, pp. 35–50.

[91]

The above set of descriptions defines politics as 'a synthetic' (or 'combinatory', 308c1) 'science', the main feature of which is its productivity. The material used by the statesman is, it seems, anthropological: the 'natural dispositions' of the citizens, who are divided into two, opposed, character groups. The *Statesman* thus regards the activity of politics and of his auxiliaries as a vast process of education which, as in the *Republic*, selects and educates its citizens. The Stranger now, in his turn, explains that those with the best dispositions will be selected in the course of tests and games, then educated in accordance with virtue, with a view to fostering unity in the city (308c–309b). But this training for excellence, which now affects all the citizens, seems to disregard the psychological aspect of the acquisition of knowledge and instead to emphasize solely the need to harmonize the movements of the different kinds of natural dispositions.[114] What needs to be done, through marriage or, better still, by inculcating citizens with the correct beliefs, is to amalgamate heavy and temperate characters with hasty and courageous ones. This operation of amalgamation, which constitutes the political 'weaving', presupposes a separation, if not a risk of incompatibility, between the diverse parts of virtue. In the *Republic*, the various virtues of the soul (and of the city) are naturally adjusted to one another. There are four in all (moderation, courage, wisdom and justice) and two of these are generally shared: moderation, which all the citizens possess, and justice, which is the virtue of harmony between the functions of a single structure. As for courage and wisdom: the former characterizes the guardians, while the latter is possessed only by those who govern. Each kind of soul thus discovers the virtue that corresponds to it, and justice is constituted by the

---

114. It is, of course, not just a matter of gymnastics. Movement (fast and slow) is here a general criterion that makes it possible to qualify the alertness of the mind as well as physical prowess. Movement is common to both the body and the soul. See, in particular, *Charmides*, 160b–d.

state of their harmonious coexistence. When the *Statesman* maintains that some of these virtues conflict, it calls into question that natural balance. To be more precise, courage is opposed to moderation, just as impetuosity is opposed to calm and quickness is opposed to slowness (306a–e). Such opposition, where virtue and conflict seemed mutually exclusive, is very surprising, in as much as it does not tally with the distinctions between the functional groups in the *Republic* and it obliges one to acknowledge that the city as a whole contains both hasty and slow characters.

It is therefore necessary to interconnect those characters, at the risk of letting them express their hostility. This way of envisaging the work of politics entails three important consequences.

In the first place, it is fair to say that, from the *Statesman* on, the conflict stems from the political analysis. Whereas the *Republic* drew a clear opposition between virtuous harmony and dissension, the *Statesman* credits the city with the ability to tolerate or even benefit from some degree of conflict between its constitutive elements. The dialogue thus makes room for conflict, instead of excluding it, and integrates it into the political creation: forging a city means getting a grip on heterogeneous material, diverse and in some cases opposed elements, and creating harmony between them. The *Statesman* in this way manages to explain the conflict of interests that governed Athenian political life, for in its own way, it was referring to the traditional opposition between the two groups in the city (the oligarchs and the democrats). Plato is no longer content to send both the Athenian 'parties' packing, and instead explains that only if they disappear (by interconnecting and merging) can a city be possible. In this way, a city can be created even out of conflicting material: existing cities can be reformed; they can be used as the basis from which to weave a fine tissue, in exactly the same way as the marriage of two opposed characters can produce characters that are harmonious.

Secondly, to encourage this interconnecting, politics must

reconcile several different kinds of activities to one another. If hostile characters are to be interlinked, they must first be educated and brought together. Politics thus retains the educational vocation assigned to it earlier, but now this is associated with institutional and technical activities that greatly extend the scope of the moulding of the citizens. First, politics must preside over the education of the citizen, but this is only a preliminary step. Once educated, the citizens are kept under observation, then submitted to a selection process (some, those who are irremediably vicious or criminal, are executed; others are reduced to slavery). Those remaining then undergo further training designed to inculcate the correct opinion or attitude, which will encourage them to live virtuously together. The nuance that distinguishes the *Statesman* from the *Republic* on this point is interesting. Plato clarifies the pedagogic part of the government's activity by suggesting that the city must undergo a special kind of education. First, citizens are trained in such a way that their respective characters emerge; then their education concentrates upon inculcating in them all 'a really true and assured opinion about honour, justice, goodness, and their opposites' (309c5–6) in such a way that all these diverse characters, being in agreement on those norms, merge together in a united effort, woven together to form a single tissue.

A third consequence is that education thus comprises two separate stages. The first is conducted by teachers, under the direction of the statesman; the second is conducted by the law. It falls to the law to weave the different characters together by means of the 'divine' bond that is constituted by the correct opinion (or attitude) that they share. The *Statesman* thus assigns to the law a specific directive function. More precisely, the law is primarily a boundary designed to prevent either of the two groups of opposed characters from straying too far from the conditions required for them to mesh. It rules out excesses, giving its material the form of a single unit (the limitation that it imposes consists

[94]

precisely in affirming the unity of a multiplicity), which is something that the citizens' education could not achieve. Between educating the citizens and assembling them by law into a single unit, there is thus a change from one kind of mathematical measurement to another, a switch from an arithmetical progression and equality (every citizen is educated) to a geometrical progression and limitation (every citizen is placed in relation to every other according to his character and activities).[115] Legislation thus sets out to play an intelligent role among the citizens. The law must understand human characters and direct them toward what is best for them. The notion that the law is endowed with thought needs to be explained.

Plato does not conceive of the law as an order, a proclamation of a governmental decision or an expression of sovereignty. For him, the function of the law is not expressive but supplementary and mimetic: the law should only be paramount in the city if its knowledgeable governor is not up to his task. In such a case—and only in such a case—the law must take over the leadership, rejecting all compromises and making no exceptions. Contrary to the Athenian idea that the law prevails because it expresses the sovereignty of the Assembly, Plato argues that the law is no more than a second-best which sets out to imitate (since it does not embody) a kind of perfection. This recourse to the law and the obligation for citizens never to contravene the laws of their city is not a sign that Plato had given up hope of a knowledgeable statesman one day existing. Rather, the argument produced in the *Statesman* sets out to support the hypothesis of knowledge that stems from thinking by

115. To understand the distinction between those two equalities, see *Gorgias*, 507a–c and *Laws*, VI, 757b–c. The distinction is one of the clearest examples of the status that Plato ascribes to mathematics in thought (both political and otherwise). As he sees it, the rationality of reality is of a mathematical nature. Purely from the political point of view, for example, mathematics is the only way of confirming the unity of that which is multiple.

showing that, even in the absence of 'a statesman', political excellence may still be within the bounds of possibility, through imitation. Even if the best possible agent to exercise the function of knowledgeable government is not available, such government may still be exercised in another fashion (albeit less knowledgeably and not as well). As Christopher Gill has explained with admirable clarity:

> Since the laws made in this way are not, by definition, based on knowledge, the 'copies' are, necessarily, not identical with (generalized versions of) the decisions that a knowledge-based ruler would make. But they represent the outcome of a cumulative process of collective attempts, under regulated conditions, to achieve the results which only the knowledge-based ruler can achieve completely.[116]

The Stranger shows the young Socrates that the law is only important and necessary in the absence of a knowledgeable authority which, if it came to exist in the city, would use the law only as one instrument among others, as one of the means available for imposing upon the city the best possible order. One of the rare laws used to establish this kind of order is, for example, that which, in the *Republic*, forbids the guardians the possession of money. However, such laws are merely a means of governmental action, just as are education, great mythical tales, cults and the exclusive practice of a single profession. The *Statesman* takes an interest in imperfect constitutions, the kind that do not realize the ultimate condition for civic perfection: namely, knowledgeable government. That is why, in the absence of such government, one has to resort to the 'royal function' that is the most effective, namely legislation (294a). It is the most effective because it alone can get diverse characters to cooperate by making them all understand one and the same

116. Gill, 1995, p. 296.

thing. What is more, whereas a myth can exert no more than a degree of persuasion where the origins or norms of behaviour are concerned, the law convinces citizens to direct their current behaviour and perform their real function in accordance with far more stringent demands. The reason why the law thus takes pride of place as a supplementary power is that it is so general and so constant. You might have thought that, in the absence of a knowledgeable man, one of the governor's aides could have fitted the bill, that in the absence of a philosopher, government could be entrusted to a judge or a general, an educator or a public speaker.

But such stopgaps are precisely what Plato seems to want to avoid for the city when he insists that it is the law that should reign in the absence of an adequate governor. His point is that the governmental function calls for an ability to know what to do in every case so as to promote the unity of the city. And none of his auxiliaries will ever possess that ability. Only the law can approximate to it. It can do so firstly because it is always addressed to the whole of the city. Even when it is ruling on a particular question and produces some prescriptive law, it is always addressed to the whole city, which is both its point of departure and its addressee (294c).[117] In the second place, it can do so because, provided it is endowed with sufficient power, it demonstrates a constancy of which no human individual has ever been capable. That is why, contrary to the belief of the Athenian democracy when it legislates in accordance with the vote of the assembly (298e), the Stranger argues that the city's laws should never be changed unless a knowledgeable governor, in all his wisdom, proves that some law or other is useless. The power accorded to the law is second-best, but it is a second-best that is adequate given the nature of the city.

---

117. Note that the unity of the city is no longer a fiction of which the citizens must be persuaded by a story (a lie), as was the case in the *Republic* (III, 414b–415c), but is now a reality, the object of legislation.

Incapable though the law is of addressing each and every citizen and seizing upon the specificity of every separate case, it can nevertheless redress the instability of the multiplicity of human affairs by the regularity of its general rules. Better a city ruled by bad laws than one ruled by incompetent governors.

Laws—and it is this, finally, that justifies their governmental status as the next best alternative—are able to imitate (but only imitate) one of the fundamental aspects of the political endeavour: namely, the ability of politics to get diverse or even hostile elements to submit to a single order. From the *Statesman* on, conflict is no longer ignored or denied, but instead is integrated into the political creation of which it becomes a living part. We can now see that the productive character of politics is not merely a consequence of the comparison of politics to the paradigm of craftsmanship; this is not just a metaphor. Politics really does produce and implant the bonds constituted by marriage and the correct attitude held by the citizens: these truly are institutions, creations of which the statesman is the author. Plato even seems to contradict himself by eventually attributing action to politics, which was earlier said to 'do' nothing (311b8). But the 'political action' evoked in the last paragraph of the dialogue still has no more than a secondary meaning since the content of that action amounts only to the fact that it orders other actions: politics is called the 'royal science' because its action consists in commanding other actions, the effect of which is to produce the woven fabric of the city. The last pages of the dialogue thus distinguish political action (which is either non-existent or mediated) from the product or creation brought about by politics which, for its part, very clearly does constitute a reality. What we should glean from all this is that, even if the statesman does not act and is not a manual craftsman (259c, the king is a theorist, he maintains his power through his strength of soul), he nevertheless does remain a craftsman who produces an object. That object is *the incorporation of the city*, that is to say the realization of the unity of all its parts, achieved in the best possible way.[118]

Laws and ways of life

It was claimed above that politics could be defined as a technique of modes of living. That is a point that is greatly illuminated by the Platonic concept of the law that is expressed in both the *Statesman* and the *Laws*. Let us now see how that concept clarifies not only how politics operates but also the material upon which the political technique works.

Right at the beginning of the long passage that Books VII and VIII of the *Laws* devote to education (788a1–842a10), the old Athenian and his interlocutors discuss the principles that ought to govern educative legislation as a whole. Their first concern is more or less the following: to what extent should one legislate with regard to education? Or rather, with respect to children, up until what age should legislation prescribe how adults should behave toward them? The Athenian's reply is famous: one needs to legislate on the behaviour of the mother as soon as she becomes pregnant, insisting that she performs certain gymnastic exercises, prior to entrusting to strong nurses the task of moving and exercising the infant's limbs as soon as it is born. If legislation is necessary from the moment of gestation onward, that is because the behaviour and activity of the mother during her pregnancy give rise to crucial consequences that affect the disposition and development of the infant, that is to say his future education and his aptitude (or lack of it) to be trained in such a way as to achieve excellence, which it is the overall function of legislation to promote. This is a formidable difficulty for the old men to tackle, and it leads on to a number of others: what should the legislator do

118. This is also the characteristic that will serve to designate the work of unification and setting in order taken on by the demiurge in the *Timaeus* (on the integration of every part, see in particular 30c–33c).

about the many seemingly unimportant habits that constitute
what is customary as regards education? What should he do,
in general, about behaviour that has become habitual and so
is now a custom (*ethos*)?[119] The question presents the task
of legislation with three problems: the first relates to the
scope of the law; the second to its material; and the third to
the relations that it may maintain with other forms of
prescriptions or norms that govern communal life. First, we
need to try to clarify the nature of these three difficulties,
before explaining how the text of the *Laws*, and before that
the *Statesman*, resolve them.

The first difficulty is how to decide upon the scope and
precise detail of the law. Two separate questions are
involved here: up to what point can one legislate, and how
precise should the law aim to be?[120] What are brought into
question here are the two facets (scope and precision) of the
possible 'exhaustiveness' of legislation. It is not the first time
the question has arisen, for it has already been posed in both
the *Republic* and the *Statesman*—a point about which there
is more below. For the time being, all that needs to be
underlined, since Plato stresses it several times in the *Laws*, is

119. Greek draws a distinction between *ethos*, custom or customary
practices, and *êthos*, an individual or collective characteristic, one's usual
dwelling or, in the plural, habitual practices or customs, *êthê*. The two
terms are clearly related and often enough are in fact synonymous. If *êthos*
has a particular connotation, it is in the sense that designates what one
might call an acquired characteristic (or even 'nature' or 'personality'),
whereas custom tends rather to qualify a repeated and habitual pattern of
behaviour. It is therefore possible to use the one term to clarify the other;
Plato does so in the *Laws*, XII, 968d2–3, when he notes that an individual
may claim to possess a skill by virtue of both his character and his habits.
Finally, Greek does, of course, make it possible to play upon the close
connection between the two words; see, for example, Aristotle,
Nicomachean Ethics, II, 1 (1103a14–18).
120. It is therefore a matter of deciding first whether all aspects of
communal life, all activities and all kinds of possessions should be subject to
legislation and then whether, where an object is subject to legislation, the
law should aim to pronounce on all or only some of its aspects or 'details'.

that the work of the legislator should cover *everything*.[121] To insist, as he does, that the law must be exhaustive and leave no human practice, no kind of activity outside the prescriptions of the law is definitely to beg the question. What Plato rules out from the start is that any activity should be authorized by silence or should lie beyond the scope of the law. It is impossible for the city to tolerate either any 'private' life that eludes the law or any activity that dodges it. On the contrary, clearly, anything not prescribed by the law is quite simply prohibited.[122] In this connection, Book X repeats that it would be absurd to neglect even subjects of scant importance and activities of a minimal nature. In similar fashion, the Stranger, using a metaphor which, as we shall see, governs the entire institution of the colony in the *Laws*, declares that, just as a mason can only build with the help of stones both large and small, similarly the legislator must also work upon small things that are few in number (902d–903b).

The second difficulty relates to the material that a legislator may or may not use. Given that the colonists expected in Magnesia will already have been educated, and also that the old men have not given up the idea of making use of whatever, in past or existing constitutions, may help them to construct their own legislation, the question that arises is that of existing norms and prescriptions that might prove useful to the law. To put that more simply, it is a matter of deciding to what extent the law may make use of ways of life and habits and even of 'unwritten' laws, in the event of such things existing.

The third and last difficulty, which is a consequence of

121. VII, 820e: the law must be, literally, 'without a single hole' (*diakena*). This is one of the points that Bertrand has emphasized in his recent study, 1999, p. 305.
122. See Aristotle's similar argument (according to which, since suicide is not authorized, it can only be forbidden), *Nicomachean Ethics*, V, 15, 1138a7 (to which Bertrand 1999, refers; p. 305, n. 263).

the second, has to do with the way in which the different kinds of prescriptions can and should be coordinated. What exactly is character of way of life (an *êthos*)? At what point does a way of life come to acquire the force of a law? Is that even a possibility? Or, to put that another way, what becomes of customs when the law is established?

The beginning of Book VII of the *Laws* resolves those three difficulties as follows: in the first place, no human practices, no modes of living should be left outside the law, abandoned to legal silence. Secondly, only the law can make customs valid, that is to say, recognize that certain customs possess an obligatory character. And finally, where modes of living are concerned, only the law can be recognized to be 'prescriptive'.

On that last point, the text could not be clearer. At 793d–e, before pronouncing on the law relating to the education of small children at the hands of their nurses, the Athenian declares that it should be applied absolutely literally (*akribôs*), not just superficially. He firmly ties the practices of nurses and teachers to the text of the law, seeming to dwell in particular upon the way in which scrupulous respect for the published text may stand in contrast to the possibly lax practice of a custom. This follows on from the elaboration of the preceding point, at 793a–d, where Plato has distinguished between a number of different kinds of prescriptive rules. What makes this text so crucial is without doubt the wide variety of the terms in play. Mention is made of *agrapha nomina*, of *patrioi nomoi*, of *patria*, and of *arkhaia nomina* and also, more generally, of *ethê*, and then of *epitêdeumata* (occupations, habitual practices, ways of doing things),[123] and *ethismata* (customs, habits)—all of which were terms that, in one way or another, the Greeks might use to designate a prescription or norm for behaviour, or the common rule.

The variety of the vocabulary definitely seems designed

---

123. To my mind, the last of these alternatives is the best translation.

to support a crucial argument, for Plato appears to be maintaining that no habit or custom, whatever the name used for it, can ever take the place of a law. He is determined to have done with all the ambiguity currently surrounding what is or is not a law in the strictest sense. The remark aimed against 'unwritten laws' implies clearly enough that, according to Plato, a law must always be written. There is nothing particularly surprising about this: after all, Plato is simply taking the measure of what the law really represents.[124] He has already done so in the *Statesman*, where he maintained that the major legislative and governmental alternative was not a matter of either written laws or unwritten ones (i.e. customs), but quite simply of the presence or absence of laws. If laws exist, they are necessarily written down, *grammata* (*Statesman*, 293a7); anything else—that is to say, the whole collection of possible customary prescriptions—has in itself no legal character at all. The *Statesman* had thus already stated that the only choice was between a scrupulous, literal respect for the laws or an absence of laws, depending on whether or not the governor needed to resort to them (292a1–2). Even though that distinction was not likely to present any difficulties, since it was thus beyond doubt that nothing was a law unless it was written, the question that did still arise, as early as the *Statesman*, was that of the respective statuses of *ethê* and *nomoi*, customs and laws, non-legal prescriptions and laws.

In the *Statesman*, Plato sets out to distinguish the statesman from all others. That is, to distinguish the knowledgeable governor from those who can be no more than his auxiliaries or those who must be regarded as his rivals. In that those auxiliaries and rivals may resemble the statesman, the question arises of the nature of resemblance and simulation (or imitation, *mimêsis*). Such reflection does indeed run right through the dialogue, but it culminates and reaches its specifically political conclusion in a discussion the subject of

---

124. As we are reminded by Bertrand, 1999, pp. 60–61.

which is, precisely, the status of the law. At this point, the *Statesman* addresses the question of whether or not to legislate when the knowledgeable governor, who is the condition and cause of the excellence of the city, is absent. In the absence of his government, should one or should one not resort to laws? As we have seen, Plato insists that one should legislate and that the laws thereby instituted should not subsequently be altered. He provides the following justification:

> *Visitor:* Yes, for if, I imagine, contrary to the laws that have been established on the basis of much experiment, with some advisers or other having given advice on each subject in an attractive way, and having persuaded the majority to pass them—if someone were brazen enough to act contrary to these, he would be committing a mistake[125] many times greater than the other, and would overturn all expert activity to a still greater degree than do the written rules.
>
> *Young Socrates:* Yes—how would he not?
>
> *Visitor:* For these reasons, then, the second-best method of proceeding, for those who establish laws and written rules about anything whatever, is to allow neither individual nor mass ever to do anything contrary to these —anything whatsoever.
>
> *Young Socrates:* Correct.
>
> *Visitor:* Well, imitations of the truth of each and every thing would be these, wouldn't they—the things issuing from those who know which have been written down so far as they can be?
>
> *Young Socrates:* Of course.[126]

(Note that this translation uses 'Visitor' where I have used 'Stranger')

---

125. The first 'mistake' would be to forbid that the law ever be changed and to forbid that the slightest activity be practised in a way other than that prescribed by the laws (299b–e).
126. *Statesman*, 300b1–c6.

This important text has been translated many times and in just as many different ways and unanimous agreement on its meaning is seldom reached.[127] I understand the last of the Stranger's three remarks to be a clarification of the second, that is to say a clarification of what good legislation should be, for, as I see it, Plato's argument is simply affirming that it is indeed necessary to legislate (in the absence of a knowledgeable government), but not to do so just anyhow: the laws must certainly be imitations of the knowedgeable constitution, *but* above all they must be made on the basis of specific forms of knowledge in each of the domains under consideration. When a law needs to be instituted, Plato insists, it must be in accordance with the indications of men who have a knowledgeable competence in that particular area. If any competent specialists or 'technicians' exist, it is up to them to advise the legislators (not just any of the citizens, as according to the belief and practice of the democrats). What the Stranger's remarks are defining when they describe the legislation as an imitation is the nature of legislative work. The legislator cannot be just anyone (a democratic Assembly, for example); he must be a knowledgeable man and, in default of the synoptic understanding of an excellent governor, he must at least possess some specific expertise or competence.

Plato insists on this point: knowledgeable expertise remains the condition for a good imitation, and that is what distinguishes good legislative constitutions from bad ones. The second remark thus clarifies the nature of legislative work and specifies who should be the *sumbouloi*, namely the qualified technicians of the existing city.[128] There are

127. Rowe, 1995b, gives a different interpretation of these pages; cf. pp. 16–17 and 230–31.
128. Immediately following the cited text, at 300c7, the true statesman is described as one who knows (*ton eidota*). This may appear to invalidate my own interpretation, which attributes such knowledge to the legislators of the second-best constitution. However, what follows in the text dissipates this ambiguity and again supports the hypothesis that good constitutions of the second rank and the excellent or correct constitution are in truth both guided by knowledge (the form of which changes, however).

therefore only two ways to imitate.[129] One is bad, with ignorant governors acting as though they were knowledgeable statesmen and consequently failing to respect the laws. The other is good, with legislation in the hands of someone with knowledgeable technical competence (see 300e1, *entekhnoi*). In this, second, case, it may not even be a matter of imitation, 'but that very thing that is most truly what it sets out to be' (300e1–2). From this we can see that what distinguishes good imitation (which is assimilation to the activity itself) from bad is, once again, the possession of a technique. That, according to Plato, is something that is lacking in the citizens of existing constitutions, so it is essential that these semblances of constitutions (*eoike politeias*), 'if they are going to produce a good imitation of that true constitution of one man ruling with expertize, so far as they can . . .—they must never do anything contrary to what is written or to ancestral customs' (300e11–301a3). Thus, what the above passage is describing is the 'good' legal imitation of knowledgeable government, and the 'men who know' who are involved are the 'inspired councillors' mentioned at 300b2, that is to say the legislators themselves.[130]

In the *Statesman*, Plato therefore proposes a juridical resolution to a major political difficulty that stems from the fact that not all citizens are knowledgeable and, above all, are not likely immediately to recognize the authority of those among them who are. (They would only be sure to do so in an excellent city with the 'correct' constitution.) The law, which Plato believes produces the correct opinions, is the means by which those governing can make known what is just (or at least ensure that this is respected). In this way it

129. Two general ways, which can then be divided into various species; see Gill, 1995, cited above in text to n. 116.
130. It is worth adding retrospectively that 259a, at the beginning of the dialogue, defines a councillor (*sumboulos*) precisely as a technician (*tekhnikês*).

is possible to make a community out of those who know and those who do not, by having those who know legislate and the other citizens govern. This is the very schema adopted in the *Laws*.[131] The last dialogue, with the problem already raised, continues the line of thought described above, on how existing customs relate to laws. The philosophical and political problem is undoubtedly the same: assuming that legislation is a kind of imitation, what should its material be, what exactly is it that must be shaped in accordance with the best model?

According to the passages from the *Laws* cited above, the question is: what should or can laws do about existing customs? Can customs be transformed into laws? Are customs the source of law? Plato replies firmly to this last question, both in the *Statesman* and in the *Laws*, rejecting the idea of recognizing that *êthos* possesses the status of a producer, or source, of law. As J.-M. Bertrand stresses:

> Whatever happens, it is up to the legislator to establish as a custom whatever has no normative force prior to being instituted as a rule. [Seen from this point of view], the Platonic formulae do not contradict the idea according to which custom is secondary to the law. Despite its alleged precedence over the law, it is only because of the law that custom is represented as the formal source of the law, whatever the effective role played elsewhere, in primitive societies, by the rules of custom.[132]

All the relevant discussions in both the *Statesman* and the *Laws* support this judgement of J.-M. Bertrand, in particular the passage at 793 in the *Laws*, the argument of which is identical to that of 298d–e in the *Statesman*, which declares that the laws of navigation must either be written down or else held to be simply unwritten ancestral customs (*agrapha*

---

131. This question is tackled by Lisi, 2000, pp. 57–82.
132. Lisi, 2000, p. 61.

patria ethê, 298e2).[133] At 793, the *Laws* again argues in
favour of reversing the old concept of custom, explaining
that it is not possible to consider customs as legal obligations
and that, on the contrary, custom must be held to *result*
from legislation. However, as J.-M. Bertrand points out, that
in no way eliminates the possibility that custom might be
regarded as one of the sources of law, or rather as part of its
material.

The question that Plato raises with regard to the law is
that of the relation that should be established between the
law and the prescriptions of custom which affect human
behaviour and which are designated by the generic category
of *êthos*. This is the category with which Plato chooses to
link the *nomina* and other *patrioi nomoi*, the better to
distinguish between, on the one hand, the whole collection of
possible kinds of custom and, on the other, *nomos*, which
should under no circumstances be confused with them.

The difficulty that now arises—one that may justifiably
seem decisive with regard to the project set out in the *Laws*
and the objective that Plato proposes there for legislation—is
that of the relationship between the law and ways of life. So
much is indicated by the rationale of the regulation about
pregnancy, which is to be found at the beginning of Book
VII: it is necessary for the law to be exhaustive, so that no
kind of custom can challenge its supremacy, for the simple
reason that infancy is the period when an individual's
character (*êthos*) is formed. The text is emphatic: 'for it is at
this age, under the effects of habit, that the whole of our
character is definitively implanted in us'. There is nothing
new about this proposition. It is almost identical to the

133. If we remember that there was at the time a political tendency that
favoured a return to the ancestral constitution, we may presume that the
argument according to which it is possible to 'produce' legislatively from the
ancestral law is, to say the least, somewhat critical. Plato seems to be
addressing to the partisans of the constitution of Solon and the 'ancestral'
laws, the overriding objection that their laws are, precisely, not laws at all.

remark already made in Book II of the *Republic*: 'Do you not know, then, that the beginning in every task is the chief thing, especially for any creature that is young and tender? For it is then that it is best moulded and takes the impression (*enduetai tupos*) that one wishes to stamp upon it'.[134]

What Plato assigns to legislation in the *Laws* is thus the educational function of character-formation which, in the *Republic*, was assigned in a more general fashion to politics. This is a very particular technical operation which is peculiarly characteristic of politics and which, accordingly, certainly does not concern only little children. If it is justifiable to describe politics as a technique, in Plato's view two things follow: in the first place, politics, like all techniques, implies the possession of some kind of knowledge, an expertise regarding its object (and also what is suitable for that object); and that is why whoever governs must understand all the objects of 'political things'[135] constituted by the citizens, their behaviour patterns, and the city institutions. Secondly, and above all, as a technician, the governor must either produce or use an object (for techniques serve either production or the use of objects).

In the *Republic*, the object that the statesman must forge, organize or mould is constituted by the customs, the *êthê*.[136] In Book IV, when Socrates defines the governmental task of the philosopher, he ascribes to him the mission of transposing or transporting into public and private customs whatever he sees up on high, in the model of excellence that inspires his political activity:

134. II, 377a12–b3, translated by Paul Shorey, Loeb Classical Library, 1956.
135. *Ta politika*: I included a number of remarks on this expression and its context in Pradeau, 1997a, pp. 110–49.
136. On this point, see again the analyses of Lisi, 2000, in particular p. 71 f., which examine the psychological conditions for the action of the law, in the *Timaeus*. To summarize, we may take it that politics is a demiurgic technique, which fashions *mores*. The latter are of a psychological nature.

'For surely, Adeimantus, the man whose mind is truly fixed on eternal realities has no leisure to turn his eyes downward upon the petty affairs of men, and so engaging in strife with them to be filled with envy and hate, but he fixes his gaze upon the things of eternal and unchanging order, and seeing that they neither wrong nor are wronged by one another, but all abide in harmony as reason bids, he will endeavour to imitate them and, as far as may be, to fashion himself in their likeness and assimilate himself to them. Or do you think it possible not to imitate the things to which anyone attaches himself with admiration?' 'Impossible', he said. 'Then the lover of wisdom associating with the divine order will himself become orderly and divine in the measure permitted to man. But calumny is plentiful everywhere.' 'Yes, truly.' 'If then,' I said, 'some compulsion is laid upon him to practise stamping on the plastic matter of human nature in public and private the patterns that he visions there, and not merely to mould and fashion himself, do you think he will prove a poor craftsman of sobriety and justice and all forms of civic virtue?' 'By no means,' he said. 'But if the multitude become aware that what we are saying of the philosopher is true, will they still be harsh with philosophers, and will they distrust our statement that no city could ever be blessed unless its lineaments were traced by artists who used the heavenly model?' 'They will not be harsh,' he said, 'if they perceive that. But tell me, what is the manner of that sketch you have in mind?' 'They will take the city and the characters of men, as they might a tablet, and first wipe it clean—no easy task. But at any rate you know that this would be their first point of difference from ordinary reformers, that they would refuse to take in hand either individual or State or to legislate before they either received a clean slate or themselves made it clean.' 'And they would be right,' he said. 'And thereafter, do you not think that they would sketch the figure of the constitution?' 'Surely.' 'And then, I take it, in

[110]

the course of the work they would glance frequently in either direction, at justice, beauty, sobriety, and the like as they are in the nature of things, and alternately at that which they were trying to reproduce in mankind, mingling and blending from various pursuits that hue of the flesh, so to speak, deriving their judgement from that likeness of humanity which Homer too called, when it appeared in men, the image and likeness of God.' 'Right,' he said. 'And they would erase one touch or stroke and paint in another until in the measure of the possible they had made the characters of men as pleasing and dear to God as may be.' 'That, at any rate, would be the fairest painting.' (*Republic*, VI, 500b8–501c3).

In the *Republic*, Plato assumes that the city, like individuals, has characteristics, (*êthê*), and that individuals' characteristics determine collective characteristics. The 'designer of political constitutions' (501c5–6) thus makes use of a divine and ordered paradigm with a view to producing human characters (*anthrôpeia êthê*) 'in the divine image'. The task of politics is to mould characters, to forge them from their earliest infancy, so in the *Laws* it is this *ethopoietic* (character-forming) function that falls specifically to legislation.[137]

In the passage of the *Laws* mentioned several times above, an important remark is made at 792e2, according to which: 'that's the age when habits, the seeds of the entire character, are most effectively implanted (*emphuetai . . . to pan êthos dia ethos*)'. Of course, Plato is playing upon the terminological affinity between character and custom but, more importantly, he is sketching in a programme which you could call a *genetic* formula for the *tekhnê politikê*: the task

137. This is one of the clearest indications that, in the *Laws*, the political technique is defined by the art of law-giving. In the *Republic*, the function of politics is to forge *customs*. The *Laws* states clearly that legislation is the suitable means for this, its appropriate tool.

of the latter, conceived as legislation, is to forge characters and customs, to bring them into being.

Politics (through legislation) must produce an accepted definition of customs. As the remark at 792e makes clear, this operation presupposes that customs play a mediating role. Laws cannot forge customs at a single stroke. Plato explains that the success of his proposal depends upon the law being transformed into custom. This is a condition that seems somewhat daunting and that, in the last analysis, itself justifies the need for the law to rule every form of human behaviour, without exception. The law cannot perform its function unless it becomes the custom in absolutely every area of life.

The chief interest of the *Statesman*, apart from its definition of political technique, lies in the way in which it undertakes to define a politics that is truly in conformity with nature (308d1), that is to say a kind of politics that satisfies the nature of the city. Through the intermediary of a technical paradigm, the city acquires the nature of a sentient object. It constitutes *the totality of the objects that the citizens are likely to use*. In the *Euthydemus* and the *Republic*, the function of politics was to educate the citizens. The organization of the city and government were either neglected (as in the *Euthydemus*) or envisaged only as one aspect of an institution that was of a partly legislative nature (as in the *Republic*). Without needing to reject the messages purveyed by those two dialogues, the *Statesman* succeeds in uniting those two aspects of the political activity in one and the same technique, the purpose of which is, precisely, the formation of the city. To conceive of the city as a specific thing, with a nature of its own, and of politics as the demiurgic activity[138] that forms it and takes care of it, in the later dialogue the Platonic doctrine is able to rest upon the cosmological and physical studies that they encompass.

138. The *demiourgos* is a craftsman. As we shall see, this is how Plato refers to the god who fashioned the universe.

[112]

Such is the importance of those studies that these last dialogues conceive of politics on the model of cosmology, They represent politics both as imitating cosmology, as an ordering submitted to the same conditions and the same explanation as the ordering of the world and also as a consequence of it, for the setting in order of the city follows on from the ordering of the world. The programme of the *Timaeus*, which is discussed next, is devoted to precisely such this idea.

4

The life of the city: the Timaeus-Critias

The world of the city

The city is a physical object, composed of heterogeneous and mobile elements that are interconnected by a technique of guidance, that is to say politics. Those who exercise the guiding function must unite those diverse, unstable, mortal elements in a single creation. They must arrange for the city to live as a single unit and for the citizens, in their turn, to live together in accordance with that essential unity. In a wide range of contexts, the dialogues of Plato present both to the eye and the mind one and the same example of a perfect arrangement of bodies: the sky. The sky is a harmonious collection of bodies whose perfection (each is spherical, and so at every point identical) renders them virtually immortal (only the god who created them could make them disappear). A celestial assembly such as this is unaffected by the vicissitudes of generation, corruption and change: the stars always remain the same. That these gods are visible is lucky for those like ourselves who do not share the same nature but can take theirs as a model for self-improvement. What is best for the nature of human beings, whether this is considered from a psychological or from a medical point of view, is a certain form of equilibrium between component parts, regularity in their respective movements and their ordering. The state of equilibrium constituted by health or thought (which requires, for example, that desires be quiescent and allow the intellect to govern us) may be achieved if we accept inspiration from the gods. The world or universe[139] is conceived as a state of physical order or structure (*kosmos*). This is what was explained in the myth with which the *Statesman* opens, when it pointed out that, even though the successive revolutions of the world regularly make most of the living beings that inhabit it disappear, the world itself never perishes: god sees to that. It is by modelling themselves on the total order in which they find themselves that physical objects can find equilibrium and know the perfection appropriate to them. The same applies to the city: even before the *Statesman*, the *Republic* set the heavens before it as a model (*Republic*, 500b–501b). This comparison between the world and the city, with the order of the latter modelled on the former, only takes on its full meaning in the *Timaeus* and the *Critias*, that is to say at the very point when Platonic doctrine gives an account of its study of the world, offering an explanation of its nature—a general cosmology and a 'physics'.

The cosmological account that takes up most of the *Timaeus* provides an explanation of how the world was made, telling how a craftsman god (the demiurge) first fashioned the soul and body of the world on the basis of the intelligible Forms, then all the living beings within it. The world is alive, an animated body, the most perfect of all physical things. It is by taking the order of the world and its mode of life as a model that the living beings that it contains become better able to participate in perfection. The cosmology and 'physics' of the *Timaeus*, which fit into the

139. The Greek word *kosmos* designates order, as well as the world, precisely because the latter is ordered.

framework of an already ancient tradition,[140] present an altogether unprecedented explanation of the creation of the world. This is the first ever demiurgic account of the creation of the world, the first craftsmanlike model of god. The fact that Plato calls his account a fiction shows, of course, that this craftsmanlike god never existed but that an attempt to explain the divine is bound to proceed in this way, constructing rational fictions that are effective enough to provide a believable representation of the nature of things under consideration. The fiction of a god looking at the Forms and using them as a model to give form to unstable and resistant material makes it possible to account both for the order and the instability of natural phenomena, and also for the 'understanding' of them that we possess.[141] This study of the nature of the world, already prepared by the modifications that the *Phaedrus* makes to the psychology of the *Republic* (by showing that the world itself has a soul and is alive through and through)[142] clearly produces consequences for the way in which the mode of life that the city constitutes is described. Both implicitly in the *Statesman* (through the presence of the myth) and then explicitly in the *Timaeus*, politics, defined as both production and usage, is conceived by Plato in the image of the ordering of the

140. Most of the writers known as 'Presocratics' or 'physiologists' contributed to a tradition of treatises *On Nature* (*peri phuseôs*), the object of which was to provide an explanation of the origin and constitution of the world. The *Timaeus* constitutes a contribution to this genre. On this question, see Naddaf, 1992.

141. The *Timaeus* provides the most complete account, before the *Laws*, of Plato's theory of knowledge or rather of the representation of the nature of the world. See Brisson, 2000b. For analyses in greater depth, see Brisson, 1998b.

142. See the eschatological and psychological myth in this dialogue (245c–249d) and the remark on the need to understand the universe as a whole in order to know what the soul is (270c).

world.[143] As for the city, this becomes one of the living things that can attain to the full perfection of which they are capable if they will only take the world as their model.

The relationship between the city and the world goes beyond mere similarity or analogy; the two entities are partly identical. What the 'physics' of the *Timaeus* declares, the explanation that it gives for the movement of bodies and for the fact, for example, that all bodies are composed from four primordial elements—all this is true of the physical things that make up the city (the land formations, the climatic phenomena, the plants and the animals, human beings included). Each of these things too, has a body, a place, and a certain movement, and some also have a soul and can think, which enables them to understand the intelligible Forms in which everything that exists participates. The city is thus part of the world. But in addition, one can say that the city is itself a world to the extent that, in imitation of the universe, it results from a craftsmanlike (demiurgic) arrangement of physical material, from which arises the constitution of an ordered whole, living its own real life.

In his last three dialogues (the *Timaeus*, the *Critias* and the *Laws*), Plato assimilates the political constraints attendant upon the ordering of human affairs to the cosmological constraints attendant upon the ordering of physical objects. He therefore no longer needs to resort to a psychological or technical comparison to define the city, but instead has the means to describe and explain both its nature, its constitution (in the physical and the political sense) and also what is best for it. The doctrinal advantage is considerable since Plato can claim to be describing precisely the

---

143. Proclus (AD 412–*c*.485) was the first of the great Platonic commentators to stress the manifest kinship between the two 'demiurgies' described by Plato—that which presides over the fabrication of the world in the *Timaeus* and that which results in the construction of the city in the *Statesman* (and in the *Critias*). See the first book of his *Commentary on the Timaeus* (there is a French translation by Festugière, 1966–68).

conditions that will or will not promote the city's excellence, rather than merely implying them by declaring, for example, that a badly governed city is vicious (a psychological meta-phor) or badly woven together (a technical metaphor). It is now possible, to state with precision that a city with a population exceeding 5,040 homes will not be viable, nor will it be viable if its territory and town are not provided with a constant water supply.[144]

So Plato introduces a political treatise at the heart of his cosmology, merging it with his 'physics' by explaining that a grasp of the nature of the world is indispensable for an understanding of the nature of a city.[145] Thus he avoids the sophistic contrast between the 'law' and 'nature' which insists that the origin of the city and the norm of justice must be attributed either to one or the other.[146] The fact that the city of the *Timaeus* is a living entity does not make it any more 'natural' than the city of the *Republic*. By nature, a human being is an animal capable, through thought, of ordering his life according to the divine image (living perfection). But there is no natural or spontaneous genesis of the city, just men who live more or less well, some like stupid brutes, others like descendants of the gods. So a choice between the law and nature does not arise; but what does arise is a choice between different ways of ordering our nature (either legally or by other means). If it is true that there is only one kind of politics 'truly in conformity with

144. These two examples, from the *Laws* and the *Critias* respectively, are not fortuitous: in Plato's day, the population of Athens exceeded that limit of 5,040 households and periodically suffered from water shortages.
145. Reading the *Timaeus* and the *Critias*, it is important not to forget that their purpose is political: the representation of the excellent city needs to be completed. It is in an attempt to do so that Timaeus explains the nature of the world, so the cosmology really constitutes the first chapter in a political work.
146. On the law-nature (*nomos-phusis*) distinction, see Guthrie, 1969, vol. 3, chs 4–5; also, Kerferd, 1981, ch. 10; also, Plato, *Protagoras*, 337c, *Gorgias* 483a–484c, *Laws*, 889a–890a.

nature', it will be the kind that is capable of rendering that nature perfect. In our case, that means politics that enables us to live united by friendship, just as the gods are. It is this difference and conflict between more or less 'natural' forms of city life that Critias explains, in his own particular way. Critias, who also appears in the *Timaeus*, follows Timaeus' cosmological exposition with all the more attention because it leads up to an explanation of human nature, which will serve as an introduction to an explanation of the nature of the city, by providing the latter with citizens. The world, human beings and the city are the three kinds of living entities that form the subject of the *Timaeus* and the *Critias*. In these dialogues, the city is not simply a collection of physical objects, but is itself a living being, a body, composed of four elements, and a soul.

The political living being

In the programme that he announces right at the beginning of the *Timaeus*, Critias sets himself the task of speaking, when his turn comes, about the nature of the city. When *Timaeus* has completed his explanation of the living being that is the world and the human living being, Critias will follow on and discuss the political living being, the nature of which can only be defined once the nature of the world and human nature have been established. So we know, right from the start, even before Critias begins to speak, that the political living being, like any other living being, possesses a body and also a soul which confers upon it movement and enables it in one way or another to understand reality. Socrates asks for the living being constituted by the city to be represented to him in movement, so that he can judge its excellence and strength. It is not a matter of just *any* city but, precisely, the one planned in the *Republic*. When he obliges Socrates to reconsider that great political discussion of his and to deplore its lack of movement and reality (*Timaeus*, 17c–19c), Plato is not calling into question the relevance of its constitution. On the contrary, he summarizes its principal features. But he is envisaging in a different way the question of its nature and its realization. For a constitution to be realized, it must be embodied in a city. Between the *politeia*, which is a plan conceived on the basis of principles, and the *polis*, which is a living being, a transformation has to take place, and that involves founding the city.[147] The foundation of the city is certainly an act of demiurgy (craftsmanship), since it presupposes a particular type of work, the assembling and moulding of various materials, and it also presupposes a history and a geography. Despite all that has been said about the absence of history in Platonic philosophy (which is sometimes alleged to recognize only cyclical time), it is clear enough that the cities evoked here do possess a history. The foundation (whether divine or human) of cities constitutes their origin: they are born, grow, acquire limits and they may clash with one another or even disappear in a flood or succumb to the blows of an enemy. That is the fate of the two warring cities in the story told in the *Critias*. The best way to set a city in motion is to push it into combat and to observe its qualities when in competition with other cities.

That is what Socrates has explained (*Timaeus* 19b–c), so that is what Critias must produce in order to satisfy him. He sets out to do so by recounting a story he heard long ago about the war which, nine thousand years previously, set his own city, Athens, against the huge empire of the island of Atlantis. But the *Critias* is unfinished: the dialogue is broken off before the war even starts and before Critias can set the two cities 'in motion'. Before that, Critias describes them both fully, one after the other. These descriptions which, under the circumstances, have to take the place of the story, are concerned with more than just the essential subject of the constitutional plan set out by Socrates in the *Republic*: the division of the citizens into functional groups. These divisions are, indeed, to be found in archaic Athens, where

---

147. *Katoikisis*, the action of installing people on a new site.

the citizens were divided into three groups. But they are mentioned only in passing, among a mass of details which focus not so much on the populations of the two cities as the land that they occupy, the resources on which they depend, and the configuration of their respective territories and towns. Before the *Laws* and for the first time in Plato's dialogues, the *Critias* presents a city plan: not an outline of the plan of a constitution, but a minute mapping of the physiology of two political bodies. The enumeration of the city's fruits and animals and the detailed description of the town planning and the architectural edifices of Atlantis are the most striking features of the *Critias*. The wealth of geographical, botanical, architectural and zoological details testifies to the fact that the nature of the city cannot be considered independently of the time and the place of its foundation. Like everything that possesses a body, the city is in a particular place; it is a particular population and a particular constitution, but also and always it is a particular site, a particular geographical setting, the land that it occupies and cultivates.

The long description of the two cities, although not followed by an account of the war between them, nevertheless does play the role that fell to Critias' discussion. The description lays sufficient emphasis upon certain parts and aspects of the two cities for it to be possible, by comparing them, to set them in opposition as two fundamental political types, two typical political natures. The one, Athens, embodies the excellence of equilibrium and lasting unity; the other, Atlantis, embodies the corruption that goes with unbalanced growth. To create these two contrary types, Critias conceives of a series of extremely explicit oppositions that enable him both to construct the two cities and to contrast them.

The features used in the description to distinguish the two cities also serve as elements in a critical analysis of the subject matter of politics. These elements fall under six categories:

[121]

- *anthropogony* how the male citizens of the city are born
- *ethnography* or rather 'sociology', for it is a matter of showing how people are distributed between the different groups, each according to a profession
- *economy* the control and use of resources
- *topography* the general geographical situation of the city and the configuration of its relief
- *chorography* the geographical aspect of the city's territory, or *khôra*, its resources and its frontiers and, finally,
- *astugraphy* or town-planning (everything to do with the town or *astu*, its organization, and its limits.

These six subject categories, set out in the same order in both cases, provide the basis for describing the two cities. Plato treats the objects that feature under these rubrics as the constitutive elements of any city. The political living entity can be defined as a body, situated in a particular place, composed of both living creatures (human beings, animals, plants) and also technical objects, and a soul which, as we shall see, is nothing other than the political *constitution*. Once again, the point that is made is that the city is not a strictly anthropological reality, not just a certain number of individuals, but also a geographical, botanical and technical reality. Once again, people performing certain activities are not the only object of politics. It is upon this preliminary point that Plato's last dialogues are most insistent.

It is worth noting that these few descriptive pages of the *Critias* are enough to set out a very specific political argument which, with a view to defining the city, combines the use of fiction (an imaginary conflict in an unknown archaic period) and that of description, as a narrative mode. The objects described are not improbable rarities or inventions, but are plausible because they are familiar. While imagining an archaic conflict, Plato speaks the language of his contemporaries, appropriating the vocabulary and methods (seeking out signs, and constructing linked, causal or circumstantial sequences) of current, historical and political discourse on the city. To describe the city, he no longer chooses to replace it with an analogue (a statue) or a paradigm (a woven fabric), nor does he resort to inventing objects or to a fiction about new languages or peoples (the people of Atlantis differ hardly at all from the Athenians except in respect of their political regime and the organization of their territory). Instead, he describes it in its material reality, enumerating its various characteristics (topographical, constitutional, economic) and its various aspects (its resources, architecture, people and army).

The cities that Critias describes do not exist, but they are described in the way that actual cities are described. Why? The most immediate purpose of Plato's story is polemical: the story is a pamphlet aimed against Athens' most recent imperialistic inclinations.[148] The sinking of Atlantis appears as a kind of bad omen, if not a threat, indicating the disaster in store for the present corrupt Athens, For the implication to be absolutely clear to the reader, it is essential that Atlantis be identified with the city of Athens, and that the reasons for its fall be made evident. That is precisely Plato's aim, as he constructs the city of Atlantis on the basis of a small number of distinctive hypotheses and features. Those features characterize Atlantis as a maritime, warmongering and imperialistic power, swept along in a movement of indefinite (excessive) expansion. The body of documentary material that Plato borrows to produce his portrait of Atlantis is designed to accentuate those features, bestowing upon them all the signs of excess. The fact that they are few

148. Between 360 and 356, the partisans of Athenian maritime and military expansion, despite defections from its allies and broken alliances, contrived to clash with those who favoured a peaceful retreat from Greek conflicts. Plato, who was hostile to the Athenian imperialistic dream, the catastophic effects of which he repeatedly denounced, supported the latter camp. For a detailed commentary on the story of Atlantis, see Pradeau, 1997a.

in number and are repeatedly stressed[149] ensures that the fictitious shift plays its polemical role and that Athens is recognizable in Atlantis. But it also enables a number of political hypotheses to come to light. The most striking feature of the story of Atlantis is that the nature, suitability and value of its distinctive features are examined *in situ*, within the framework of a rational fiction[150] that tests them out as hypotheses from which it can deduce certain consequences.

Although this type of 'rational fiction' certainly proceeds in a programmatic fashion to the extent that its message is believable, it nevertheless remains unrealizable. We remain in the familiar realm of the discursive rational construction of a political constitution. The aim of the philosopher-statesmen who found cities is never to apply their plans in a strict, mimetic fashion, for those plans are only *types*.[151] However, the fact that no direct realization of the rational fiction is to be expected in no way presupposes that it is a useless fiction: for it does have a possible use[152]—a use for the man who must rule the city and, in order to do so, must know what is best for it. In this sense, as Socrates and Critias both suggest,

149. The repetition is thematic. The description of Atlantis is full of recurrent motifs, each of which refers to a plurality of themes (maritime and military, but also matters to do with horses or the decorative arts) and all of which emphasize that the island loves money and luxury, encourages a culture of ornamentation and grandiloquence, and is obstinately turned toward the sea and commerce—all passions that must inevitably have had a familiar ring for the Athenians.

150. Such as the cosmological model produced by Timaeus, which Critias proceeds to imitate.

151. The use of this term seems preferable to that of the vaguer 'model' for designating a rational instrument of knowledge obtained by the theoretical construction of a schematic picture possessing no historical relevance but able to test and elucidate the notions used in political analysis. This idea and the above definition are of Weberian inspiration.

152. It is the use to which Clinias refers in the Laws, III, 701d, where he says that a 'reasoned' constitution is helpful both when examining existing cities and when founding a future city.

the memory of this archaic conflict may be said to be *true*. Similarly, precisely because the story is no more than a seemingly true representation, it may be applied to a number of different but similar realities.[153] The story of Atlantis thus serves a political project the aim of which is not only polemical but also foundational. It presents two typical forms of organization based upon analogous distinctive features (relating to the organization of the population and the shaping of the territory), but also based on different patterns of development in those two societies. Here is a detailed plan of the account:

Timaeus (20d8–27b6)
20d8–25d7: what Critias remembers
    20d8–21d9: preamble. Critias remembers the elder Critias telling the story
    21e1–25d6: the elder Critias' story (Solon and the priest)
        21e1–23d4: Saïs and ancient memories
        23d4–25d6: the finest Athenian exploit
25d7–26c5: Critias recalls the story
26c6–26e2: Critias responds to Socrates' request
26e3–27a1: Socrates agrees
27a2–27b6: the programme of the *Timaeus* and the *Critias* (to describe the world, humanity and the city)

Critias (106a1–112e7)
106a1–106b8: Timaeus is invoked
106b9–109a8: prologue and summary
109b1–112e7: Athens
    109b1–109d2: the divine selection of the place and the government of the autochthonous souls

---

153. The fact that Plato constructs a single fictitious type means that he does not need to choose between the available Athenian, Persian, Syracusan, Egyptian or even Cretan referents. By basing his description of Atlantis on various aspects of them all, he creates a belligerent imperial type that suffices to pass judgement on them all, using the yardstick of the criteria deployed.

109d2–110d5: the autochthonous inhabitants
110d5–111e5: the territory of Athens
111e5–112d3: the town
112d4–112e7: the number and the government of the guardians

Atlantis (112e7–121c4)
113a1–113b6: a remark on the names in the story
113b7–114d8: the divine selection of the place and the engendering of the population
114d8–115b6: the resources
115b7–118e7: the organization of the island
118e7–119b8: the military forces of Atlantis
119c1–120d5: the royal power
120d6–121c4: the moral decline of Atlantis

As has been noted above, the construction of the types of political organization described in the *Critias* is inseparable from the cosmological exposition in the *Timaeus*. That is not only because the city is a reality in the world, but also and above all because it is a living reality. That is why the *Critias* can discourse on the city using the terms and explanations that the *Timaeus* applies to the nature of every living entity. The 'general' physiology (which applies both to man and to the world) of the *Timaeus* is designed to make possible and to define the political physiology of the *Critias*.

That general physiology defined the health of a living entity, of whatever kind, as a dynamic equilibrium that is the sole remedy for all diseases: 'neither to exercise the soul without the body nor the body without the soul so that they may be evenly matched and sound of health' (*Timaeus*, 88b6–c1). Health is a dynamic equilibrium that only the soul can produce by imposing its own motion upon the six different movements of the body. Timaeus' anthropology can thus define human nature as a whole composed of two parts, each of which has the ability to move in ways that need to be kept in order, that is to say coordinated and controlled. This is the composite human nature that Critias takes over and of which he goes on to give a mobile and political representation. He does, however, point out that the men whose archaic conflict he hopes to relate had first been distinguished by the education they had received. That is to say, precisely by one of the two principal means of promoting the equilibrium of human living beings that Timaeus has indicated (87a–c), the second being the political constitution under which a man lives and is educated. The men and women in Critias' story (the ancient Athenians) have received the most excellent of educations: they are, remember, the citizens of Socrates' *Republic* (*Timaeus*, 18a–c). The *Critias* is certainly thus presented as a re-reading of the *Republic* in the light of the study of the world and people produced in the *Timaeus*.

The story of Atlantis is thus designed to constitute a revision of Plato's political doctrine in the light of the cosmology and anthropology set out in the *Timaeus*. A project of exhaustive enquiry is announced which, on the basis of the cosmological explanation, will be in a position to define the nature of human and political things. The same instruments of analysis and the same explanatory models will be used for both. This means, in particular, that the political reflection that governs the *Critias* must consider whether it is possible to institute a dynamic equilibrium in the domain of human and mortal affairs. It also explains why, after representing the total living entity and the human living entity, the enquiry *into nature* devotes itself to the political living entity. The merit of this hypothesis is that it makes sense of the profusion of descriptions, lists and measurements in the dialogue.

In order to demonstrate the corporeal nature of physical things, the *Timaeus* described their elementary physical constitution in geometrical terms, and then went on to explain their movements (for instance, those involved in attraction, composition and dislocation). Critias clearly bears that description in mind. When reading the *Critias*, one is struck

[127]

by the fact that the narrative part of the dialogue is entirely taken up by Atlantis; without it, there would be no war, no story. The reason for this is simple: Atlantis *expands*. As most commentators have pointed out, it is in movement, whereas Athens remains immobile. But it would be more accurate to say that Athens keeps moving on the spot (its citizens are not at rest but work on the land and at their various skills), whereas Atlantis is constantly altering its boundaries and the configuration of its territory by multiplying its divisions and the works (mostly hydraulic) undertaken there. This movement of expansion is discontinuous and irregular: it is neither centrifugal, nor uniform, nor homogeneous. An examination of the geometric figures relating to volume in Atlantis shows that, despite the abundance of measurements, a morphological incoherence persists. For example, the congruence of the five concentric rings drawn by Poseidon around the central mountain is shattered by his royal descendants, who pierce them with a rectangular canal (113d–e and 115c–d). Also, to take another example, far from being gathered together in the same place, as the Athenians are, the citizens of Atlantis are *distributed* among the various towns and villages, which are separated by ramparts, gates or canals. In general, two kinds of configuration are set in contrast in these descriptions: circular figures which, as is well known, envelop, contain and limit physical objects (where the sphere of the world is concerned),[154] and rectangular figures which, when composed, do not fit together spontaneously and are all liable to become corrupt. The unity of Athens (a city) and the imbalance of Atlantis (a vast colonial empire) are contrasted precisely from the point of view of the limits indicated by their respective frontiers. As the copious detail devoted to geographical frontiers shows, a limit is what determines and defines what it circumscribes.[155]

154. *Timaeus*, 33b f.
155. See in particular *Philebus*, 25d f.

For these two cities, a limit is not always a matter of frontiers; it may consist in the territorial and architectural configurations that circumscribe the framework of life and the activities of the citizens. From this point of view, Atlantis is not so much limitless as excessively limited: volumes abound and juxtapose square limits (the districts), rectangular ones (the plain, but also the temples and the canals) and circular ones. Instead of being surrounded by a single circle, that is to say contained and defined, there are many different kinds of configurations and it is not possible for bodies all to be subject to the same movement,[156] so that the territory of Atlantis is swept by movements as numerous as they are diverse and limitless. There is but one limit: the sea. This is not a political limit, for it succeeds neither in uniting nor in defining the territory and city that it surrounds. Atlantis is a city without equilibrium. The catastrophe of Atlantis, predictable ever since the description of the island, will be the physiological result of the pronounced imbalance of its constitution. But the excessive resources of Atlantis are not just an artificial and redundant illustration of the immoderation that is engulfing it; they are, in a very real sense, bodies that politics now needs to cope with. If the function of politics, in order to prevent the city from foundering in immorality and injustice, is to set in order and set a limit on bodies, its task must be to envelop *all* the bodies contained within the city limits (and therein lies the reason for the failure of Atlantis). Politics, in conformity with the demiurgic character conferred upon it by the *Statesman*, must govern the use of all resources and all products. The interest of the *Critias* lies in the way that it sets that task in a local context, disposing in relation to one another and within the limits of a common territory all the forms (technical, urban and architectural devices) that must promote the equilibrium of the human beings living there.

156. See above all the example of the plain of Atlantis, a jumble of all kinds of figures (118a–119a).

Accordingly, the physical material set in order (or 'woven together') in the description of the cities of the *Critias* is even more vast than the arts and products envisaged in the *Statesman*. In the *Critias*, politics takes into account the *totality* of the bodies and objects likely to relate to human affairs (the geographical situation, the climate, the botanical plants grown for food and so on). A city may be defined within precise geographical limits, according to the use that it makes of all its resources. The justice and excellence of ancient Athens can thus easily be appreciated simply by observing how well the knowledge of its cultivators and craftsmen is adjusted to (or suits, 111e) the prodigality of the land.

These remarks should help us to understand the role that Plato ascribes to the city plans discussed in his last two political dialogues (the *Critias* and the *Laws*). Far from being simply suggestions as to the form that the administrative and functional divisions of the city territory should take, these plans constitute political responses to a physiological and dynamic problem. Devising a city plan is a matter not so much of dividing the city into different functional quarters, in the manner of Athenian town planning, but rather of undertaking to limit and control the movements of the bodies of which the city is composed.[157] So it is not so much the geography or the town planning as such that interest Plato, but rather the local limitation of the movements of the city and all its parts. In the circular city of the *Laws*, the greatest attention is paid to the regular movements of the groups of citizens from one portion of the territory to another (pp. 156–62 below).

157. This is exactly the explanatory hypothesis upheld, in a different way, in the *Statesman*, which explains that the function of the royal weaver is to enmesh and link together characters that are lively and characters that are sluggish (308c–311c). The same explanation reappears in the *Critias*, and is extended to all the bodies that affect human and political life or make it possible.

The Athens of the past, the fortunate choice of Hephaestus and Athena, was a territory naturally suited to virtue and to thought (109c10–11). But that suitability stemmed from the coincidence of the excellence of the land and the excellence of the Athenians. The former offered the latter all the means of subsistence, the best of every kind (plants and animals, construction materials and climate). The citizens, for their part, in conformity with the terms of the *Timaeus*, cited above, exhibited a perfect combination of body and soul (112e6) that enabled them to profit from the perfection of their territory. The physiology of Athens resulted from those two forms of excellence, the one natural, the other anthropological. The city occupied an immense acropolis, a circular hilltop on the summit of which the guardians lived and governed and around which the craftsmen and cultivators lived and worked. The body of the city possessed natural fixed limits that surrounded a finite number of bodies (112e, the human population was fixed, and resources were regularly and consistently extracted).[158] The difficulties inherent in maintaining control over movements appeared to be resolved all the better given that no new body ever seems to have been able to be added to the city. In this way it reserved its morphology and its equilibrium right up to the point when an earthquake, a catastrophe alien to its nature, destroyed it.

The *Critias* completes the *Timaeus*, making the two dialogues a coherent whole, a single enquiry in which the three successive objects are the world, humanity and the city. The incompleteness of the enquiry does not prevent our understanding its plan and its principles. Proceeding from the hypothesis that those three objects are all living entities

---

158. It should be noted that the strict limitation of the Athenian territory by no means prevents the city from governing all the other Greek cities (112d). This means that the perfection of its nature (ordered and closed) is the cause of its superior power. In Plato's political doctrine, self-sufficiency and hegemony are not contrary terms.

with a similar corporeal and psychic nature, the enquiry sets out to submit the definition of their nature, their constitution, and their development to the same kind of analysis. To define a living entity is to describe its basic constitution, its movements, and the equilibrium that it is capable of achieving. This is the task that falls to physiology (here understood as the science of nature, or rather *an enquiry into nature*), in which the *Critias* is merely the chapter devoted to politics. But, although the physiology of politics does not call that in question, it does introduce an important new element into the doctrine expounded in dialogues prior to the *Statesman*, when it describes the city as a physical individual entity. What the *Republic* presents only as an analogy and what the *Statesman* describes only from the technical aspect finds its full representation in the story of Atlantis: it is now possible to define the city as a living entity of a particular kind. This is exactly what Socrates wanted (that his city should at last be given life, *Timaeus*, 19b–c), and it is what he gets in the *Critias* at the cost of making an unprecedented alteration in the mode of the city's generation: by being delimited, encompassed and determined by boundaries, the political totality is truly engendered, as a mixture of divine and mortal parts.

Plato's philosophy is thus able to give an account of the nature of the city. But perhaps it is no longer just a matter of *political* philosophy: in the *Timaeus* and the *Critias* the city, positioned in between the world and humankind, acquires a status and dignity that the *Republic* had barely envisaged. The city is a subject that requires specialist knowledge. The *Laws* give that suggestion the support and illustration that can only be provided by a truly systematic work.

5

The city, a world of politics:
the Laws

Diogenes asked Plato if it was true that he had written the
Laws, and went on to ask, 'So what was the problem?
—for you also wrote the *Republic*.' 'Certainly.' 'Well, is
the *Republic* devoid of laws?' 'Not at all.' 'Then why did
you have to write the *Laws* as well?' (Stobaeus, III, 13,
45).

The *Timaeus* and the *Critias* constitute the necessary
condition and preparation for a systematic philosophical
work that Plato was either unable or unwilling to realize in
that form. The *Laws*, which returns to and completes
the programme designed for the trilogy constituted by
the *Timaeus-Critias-Hermocrates*, is neither a legislative
treatise nor even simply a work of 'political philosophy'. It
completes the systematic project behind Plato's whole
oeuvre, for in this dialogue he tackles every aspect of
the reality of which philosophy sets out to give an
account.

Over recent years, this last, unfinished work by Plato
has been the object of a renewed interest. Nowadays the
Laws is much discussed, although the dialogue has not
yet been the subject of a thorough exegesis or an overall

interpretation.[159] It is true that the length of the text is somewhat daunting, but that only partly explains the reticence and lack of impetus displayed by commentators. It is surely not just because the *Republic* is one hundred pages shorter that it is the more widely read dialogue. It is certainly surprising that the *Laws*, for the very reason that it is such an imposing text, hardly attracts more attention than the tiny *Critias* and the brief *Apology*. The explanation no doubt lies in the inherent interest of those two dialogues. The reticence of commentators seems proportionate to the boredom of readers, for both are misled by the legislative arsenal of a body of work so vast that when, in the eighth book, one comes across the rules relating to the right time to harvest grapes and figs, one hardly remembers that the work's initial purpose was to enquire into the best way of governing a city.[160] Commentators thus tend to come to terms with both their boredom and their seemingly well-founded impression that the very text of the *Laws* is not always up to the obviously high standard of the other dialogues; so they settle for a partial study. Alternatively, they distance themselves from the dialogue by concentrating on the question of whether, for example, it is earlier than the others or not, whether it echoes the *Republic* more than the *Statesman*, or whether, or whether, finally, it might show *a posteriori*,

159. There are some exceptions: among them the comprehensive reading of the dialogue produced by Piérart, 1974, and above all, unknown to the above author, the long chapter on the *Laws* by Netschke-Hentschke, 1971. See also the commentary by Stalley, 1983. Since the early 1980s, the bibliography has grown considerably; see details for the 'Bibliographie Platonicienne' in the introductory note to my bibliography.

160. Yet it is juridical and penal aspects that the major commentaries on the *Laws* have addressed. Among contemporary publications, most of the more interesting studies stem from the history of law and try to explain Plato's choices by comparing them to the law of various Greek cities (essentially, most of Plato's borrowings turn out to be Athenian). Three texts stand out from this critical literature: Gernet's long introduction to the Laws, 1951, vol. I, pp. xciv–ccvi; Morrow's commentary, 1960; and the more detailed study by Saunders, 1991.

that the *Timaeus* was produced before the *Statesman*.[161] Among those thematic studies and those chronological speculations which, in the end, contribute nothing new to our understanding of the *Laws*, there is surely room for a serious interpretation of the *Laws*. The remarks below will, I hope, make a useful contribution to that interpretation.

The laws of the constitution

Might the *raison d'être* for the weighty body of legislative discourse that readers find so boring in the *Laws* be a serious decision that Plato took, following all the personal betrayals and disappointments that his own catastrophic political experiences afforded him? Is it the case that the *Laws*, written by a disillusioned philosopher many years after the theoretical excellence of the *Republic* and after the *Statesman*, constituted an attempt to set the city within the context of the unpredictable and imperfect circumstances of becoming, or history: accidents, human weaknesses and ignorance, and their inevitable complement of approximations and mistakes? Did the ageing Plato come to realize that a statesman cannot dispose of his material as he wishes to, and so eventually concede the government of the city to the second-best instrument constituted by the law? Such a biographical interpretation, which is long-standing but false,[162] is based

161. I am here alluding to the hypotheses of Owen, 1965, pp. 313–38. Those hypotheses are, however, refuted by Cherniss in the same volume, pp. 339–78, but they continue to arouse the curiosity of certain interpreters. See also Gill, 1979.

162. Its origin is probably modern, for it is already to be found in Marsilio Ficino, as is noted by Neschke, 1995 (preface). Of all the contemporary commentators, Neschke is the one who has the most vigorously challenged the hypothesis of the philosophical and political 'disappointment' of Plato in his old age. She believes, on the contrary, and with good reason, that the *Laws* may be considered the most characteristic expression of Plato the philosopher. It is a dialogue that testifies to a life and thought that is all of a piece and is dominated by one fundamental motif: to know what is good and to make it happen (1971, p. 324). In the same vein, see the fifth section of Neschke, 1995, pp. 137–64.

on a confused comparison between the *Laws* and the *Statesman* and on the hypothesis that Plato gave up the idea of a perfectly knowledgeable governor (a monarch who has become a philosopher, or vice versa) and settled for a legislative stopgap, that of the all too famous 'second-best'.[163] It is also based on all the Sicilian disappointments that Plato is assumed to have suffered—those related in Letter VII.[164] In the last analysis, it reduces Plato's dialogue to a lengthy work all the more useless and tedious because it bears the stamp of disillusionment: 'the degree of compromise with the material world is far greater than what we find in the *Republic* . . . In comparison to his other works, Plato's mood in the *Laws* is definitely sinister'.[165] Recent interpreters have tried to correct this reading of the *Laws*, stressing either the doctrinal originality of certain passages (which amounts to saying that the book contains a speculative element), or else the impressive attempt at clarification and systematization that dominates the treatment of its principal chapters.[166] They have, for instance, in particular drawn attention to the great effort that Plato makes in the

163. This is the 'second option' mentioned in the *Statesman*, 300a–c, which explains that, in the absence of the best constitution, respect for the laws of the existing constitution must be maintained. The main relevant passages in the *Laws* are 691a–b, 713c–714a, 875c–d. See further (sceptical about this reading of the evidence), Gill, 1995, pp. 301–4.

164. 325c f. But those who believe this letter to be authentic should pay attention to what the author actually says. He mentions setbacks but expresses no renunciation of his views and retains the idea that excellence is the objective of politics.

165. This, the most generally shared diagnosis, is put forward by Klosko, 1986, pp. 198 and 199. For a similar presentation of Plato's 'final failure', see already Piérart, 1974, pp. vii–viii. Finally, see also, recently, 'the tendency to empiricism that appears in the *Laws*' as described by Annas, 2000.

166. For example, Saunders's detailed study of the coherence and originality of the penal material (1991) and Naddaf, 1992, in which he shows that the *Laws* constituted the final phase of Plato's research *into nature*.

Laws to accommodate the irrational factor that so bedevilled the *Republic*, and hence to promote the foundation of a 'mixed' constitution of a kind that allows irrational desires to continue to exist, thanks to their being legally subordinated to the demands of reason.[167] That is how it is that the law can accommodate modes of behaviour and beliefs that would never have found a place in the *Republic*.

Most of these interpretations and studies are still in progress, but they will eventually be completed. Even so, they will not necessarily dispel the previous assumptions that this text will be a tedious read. That is why, rather than strive to clarify the traditional interpretation of the *Laws*, I will call it into question entirely, arguing instead that in its last stages, Plato's philosophy is an *adventurous* one that resolves problems that the *Republic* did not seem able to tackle. For example, the development of the city, its body, the conflicts that may disrupt it, and the modes of behaviour of its citizens. Because the last dialogues (the *Timaeus*, the *Critias*, and the *Laws*) rest upon a fully worked-out 'physics', which makes it possible to define the elements and movements of all physical things, they are in a position to elaborate a doctrine that has the capacity to account for reality as a whole—the reality that is the world. The 'theory' of the *Laws* thus does not give up on 'reality' but on the contrary claims to explain it. To gain recognition for this view and to contribute to a fairer interpretation of the last dialogue, remember first that the *Laws* continues directly in the line of Plato's constitutional enquiry into the most excellent of cities. The only difference is that the *Laws*, following on from the *Critias*, not only describes the constitution of the city, but furthermore defines it as a living entity.[168] Next, I shall try to show that the *Laws* put the

167. For example, see Bobonich, 1991.
168. The kind of knowledge that focuses upon this living entity is a 'political physiology'. With regard to the *Critias*, I explain this zoological status of the city in Pradeau, 1997a, p. 282f.

[137]

finishing touches to understanding the city from the point of view of its political physiology. Lastly, I shall discuss the possible relationship between Plato's systematic explanation of reality and his plan for the foundation of a city.

The purpose of the *Laws* is identical to that of the other Platonic dialogues that discuss the city, above all the *Republic*.[169] As in that dialogue, the aim ascribed to political thought and the planning of the city's constitution and government is to enable all the citizens to gain access to virtue in its entirety. And, in the *Laws*, as in all Plato's dialogues, this is only possible in a city ruled by intelligence. What this enquiry sets out to do is thus, once again, to plan a well-governed city, within the order of discourse guided by reason.[170] However, this dialogue, right from the start, is concerned to specify the identity of the founder(s) of the projected city. Those who found the city, whether they are the interlocutors of the *Laws* or the colonist leaders of whom they speak and to whom they in advance address their discourse, are 'legislators'. This specification is crucial, for only if we understand what the *legislative* function is can we understand the object and the status of the *Laws*. The legislator is the man who forges the constitution, the one who institutes the city. So he is not simply a composer of the law, as a modern member of the legislative body is. He is the founder of both the constitution and, along with it, the city.[171] In the situation envisaged by the *Laws* (a colony is about to be founded, from scratch), the legislator is a founder: he creates the institutions and regulates them,

169. Aristotle, who repeatedly criticizes the *Laws* (*Politics*, II, 2 to 6) does not regard the dialogue as a different literary genre (both the *Laws* and *Republic* are treated as treatises on the constitution), nor as a different argument (there are more laws in the *Laws*, Aristotle says, but in the last analysis the constitution is the same).

170. *Laws*, III, 702d1–2 and e1–2, and V, 736b5–6, which use the formula in the same way as in the *Republic*, II, 369a6–8 and c9, and also at 376e1.

171. The Athenian, who leads the discussion in the *Laws*, stresses the unusual nature of this definition of legislation, I, 630d f.

which means that he also governs the city. But before studying the way in which the legislator founds and governs, a word needs to be said about the status of his work and the general aspect of the dialogue.

The constitution of the city

Initially the *Laws* simply takes over where the incomplete duo formed by the *Timaeus* and the *Critias* left off. In particular, it provides a history of the development of cities from the time of origins (the flood) down to the then present day (at the beginning of Book III). Following on from the birth of the world (cosmogony) and that of mankind (anthropogony) described in the *Timaeus*, the *Critias* first, and then the *Laws*, move on to describe the birth of the city (politogony).[172] But the *Laws* then complements its polygony by an institutional and historical analysis of four contemporary powers: Crete, Sparta, Persia and Athens. The dialogue thus presents an apparently heterogeneous aspect, a jumble of myths of origin, poetic stories and recent history. A plan of the *Laws* sorts this out. A preamble that defines the function of the law (to constitute a city that will be the best possible: I, 624a1–628e1) is followed by a first section that is devoted to an examination of all the types of possible constitutions (I, 628e2–III, 702e2) and a second devoted to a description of the virtuous city (IV, 704a1–XII, 968e5). All this is rounded off by an epilogue (XII, 968e6–969d3).[173] The general plan of the dialogue is thus that of a very straightforward demonstration. The interlocutors discuss the best way of constituting a city. The task falls to legislation;

172. We may therefore assume that Plato deliberately abandoned the unfinished *Critias* in order to write the *Laws*, which return to and complete the programme described at the beginning of the *Timaeus*. That is the hypothesis that I defend in my conclusion to Pradeau, 1997a.
173. Many textual difficulties and approximations do, however, show that the dialogue is unfinished, the apparent reason for this being Plato's death.

but present and past legislation provides no example that satisfies the demands of perfection. So the very best of cities must be constructed by discourse, created by reason. And that is what the *Laws* does.

I, 624a1–628e1: Preamble: the law must constitute the city in accordance with the greatest good

I, 628e2–III, 702e2: the object of legislation: a virtuous city

    I, 629a1–II, 674c7: A. *the aim of legislation*

        629a1 f.: neither the legislation of Crete nor that of Sparta aims at total virtue

        632d8–636e3: different types of virtue

        636c4–674c7: controlling pleasures (education and drunkenness).

        The law is the best instrument for controlling pleasures and modelling souls

    III, 677a8–702e2: B. *the origin of constitutions*

        677a8–693c6: cities after the flood

        693c7–702e2: the two constitutional types: Persia and Athens.

        To date there has been no virtuous city

IV, 704a1–XII968e5: Constituting the virtuous city

    IV, 704a1–V, 734e5: A. *preamble*

        704a1–715e6: presenting the city: its location and the origin of the colonists

        715e7–718a6: an address to the colonists

        718a7–719e7: recommendations for the legislator

        719e8–734e5: the nature, function and content of the principal preambles

    V, 734e5–XII, 968e5: B. *the laws of the constitution are set out*

        734e5–768d7: 1. preliminaries: the city and its magistracies

           the purification of the city

           the population and sharing out the land

           a clarification of the three ranks of excellence for a city

the number of households
an exhortation to respect these measures
wealth
the division of the territory
the magistracies and their duties
VI, 768d7–XII, 960b5: 2. the establishment of the laws
introduction
households
marriages and domestic goods
education
food and resources
crimes and punishments
properties and contracts
secondary wrongs and offences
the controllers
the oath and fines
relations with foreigners
various offences
courts of law
funerals
XII, 961b6–968e5: 3. safeguarding the laws: the council
XII, 968e6–969d3: Epilogue

The first part of the *Laws* addresses each of the possible types of constitution: those that existed in the past, those said to have existed and those existing in the present.[174] And in the case of each example, the interlocutors ask themselves whether or not it made possible the realization of total virtue for the whole city. In every case the answer is in the negative, for not one of the constitutions examined favoured more than partial virtue (not total virtue) or virtue for more than some of the citizens (not for the whole of the city). Understandably then, since neither history nor myth satisfy

---

174. See the remark made in IV, 714b ('How many constitutions are commonly recognized we have recently recounted'), which reminds us that this lengthy enquiry is a *constitutional typology*.

the conditions laid down at the start, it is necessary to resort to a rational fiction, to create a fictional constitution. This creation must discover how to remedy the defect diagnosed in the conclusion to the first enquiry of the *Laws*: to this day no city has been virtuous for none has managed to live in accordance with reason, or intellect (*nous*). The founders of the virtuous city (its legislators) will therefore have to forge and administer their city *intelligently*, with a perspective which is explicitly that defined in the *Republic*: there can be no excellence, no perfection except with and through thought. Unlike the *Republic*, however, which left the problem unresolved, the *Laws* attributes to the founders, as the legislators of the city, a special instrument for governing. This, of course, is the law.

In the *Laws*, the law is *instrumental and constitutive*: the law is the proper means used by the legislator to found the city and set it in order.[175] To use Plato's own terms and wordplay more precisely, the law (*nomos*) is the instrument of the intellect (*nous*).[176] The elliptical definition that the *Laws* provides is the following: the law is a 'distribution of reason' (IV, 714a2) in the sense that, through it, reason determines modes of conduct, and also in the sense that reason effects a distribution (a sharing out of what is due to each individual in the city).[177] This function, at once prescriptive and distributive, of the intellect will be familiar enough to readers of the *Republic*, for it is precisely the function performed by that dialogue's founders of the best of all cities when, for example, they selected from among the guardians those that were to practise dialectic and to

175. As I have indicated in Pradeau, 1997a, it is in the *Critias* that this new use of the law first appears (pp. 298–304).
176. The wordplay appears at IV, 714a and XII, 957c.
177. Bobonich, 1991, discusses the first aspect of the matter (rational persuasion) and defends a rhetorical concept and use of the law. The second aspect (distributive justice) is the subject of Neschke, 1995 (see in particular lecture V and the overall conclusion). The two aspects should be considered together.

govern.[178] Here, in the *Laws*, the law assumes that same constitutive function, in the strongest sense of the term, for it is the laws which, all added together, give the city its constitution, its rules, its limits and finally, its mode of life.[179] There is, then, no difference between the legislative technique and the political activity that founds and governs the city. In the *Laws*, the legislative technique is simply another name for politics.[180] Of course, the replacement of politics by the legislative technique calls for an explanation. In the *Statesman*, the law was just a function, one means among others of exercising the governmental technique — a means that only became essential as a principle of government when the city was without a knowledgeable governor (297b f.). The perspective of the *Laws* is quite different, for here legislation seems to constitute the whole of politics, and furthermore co-exists with a knowledgeable legislator-governor, or rather with a knowledgeable legislating-and-governing function.[181]

For, to be well administered, the city does not need such or such a legislator or the intellect of any particular individual; what it needs is for intellect, as such, to preside over the disposition of its material and its organization.

178. See VII, 534e f.; the work of selection (distribution) is described in terms that serve to define the function of the law in the *Laws*.
179. To put the city in order, to organize it, is to put its laws in order (IV, 712b).
180. Legislation and politics are taken to be synonymous, at II, 657a, and again V, 742d–e. See also *Republic*, VI, 502b–d.
181. It is important to point out, once again, that the political figures whose skills are described in Plato's dialogues only receive their names and titles in relation to their *functions*. Plato defines functions and skills, not anthropological qualities or personal characteristics. If rulers must also become philosophers (or vice versa), that is because the function of government requires a knowledgeable administrator. If a statesman is a craftsman who envelops the city in a single tissue, that is because the political technique must lie in the production of just such a tissue. Unlike his successors, Plato never wonders who can or should govern the city, but invariably asks simply *what must be done* for the city.

Whether that function is exercised by means of legislation or by government by a person (a knowledgeable tyrant) in the end hardly matters; in fact, if it came to a choice, the *Laws* would opt for legislation because it does not suffer from the defect inherent in the nature of every human character: corruption. The interpreters who go out of their way to stress the absence of 'philosopher-rulers' in the *Laws* (but did they really ever exist even in the *Republic?*) clearly do not see that Plato never makes the government of the city a matter of *personalities*. It is with just such an attitude that the Athenian, who leads the discussion, establishes a hierarchy that has become all the more famous because it is usually understood to be Plato's way of acknowledging that he has given up the idea of political perfection. In this passage (from Book V), however, the Athenian contents himself with showing that the model to which the human city should conform is that of the gods, which perfectly realizes what human beings can only strive to achieve.

> The next move in this game of legislation is as unusual as going 'across the line' in checkers, and may well cause surprise at first hearing. But reflection and experience will soon show that the organization of a state is almost bound to fall short of the ideal. You may, perhaps—if you don't know what it means to be a legislator without dictorial powers—refuse to countenance such a state; nevertheless the right procedure is to describe not only the ideal society but the second and third best too, and then leave it to anyone in charge of founding a community to make a choice between them. So let's follow this procedure now: let's describe the absolutely ideal society, then the second best, then the third. On this occasion we ought to leave the choice to Clinias, but we should not forget anyone else who may at some time be faced with such a choice and wish to adopt for his own purposes customs of his native country which he finds valuable.
>
> You'll find the ideal society and state, and the best code

of laws, where the old saying 'friends' property is genuinely shared' is put into practice as widely as possible throughout the entire state. Now I don't know whether in fact this situation—a community of wives, children and all property—exists anywhere today, or will ever exist, but at any rate in such a state the notion of 'private property' will have been by hook or by crook completely eliminated from life. Everything possible will have been done to throw into a sort of common pool even what is by nature 'my own', like eyes and ears and hands, in the sense that to judge by appearances they all see and hear and act in concert. Everybody feels pleasure and pain at the same things, so that they all praise and blame with complete unanimity. To sum up, the laws in force impose the greatest possible unity on the state—and you'll never produce a better or truer criterion of an absolutely perfect law than that. It may be that gods or a number of the children of gods inhabit this kind of state: if so, the life they live there, observing these rules, is a happy one indeed. And so men need look no further for their ideal: they should keep this state in view and try to find the one that most nearly resembles it. This is what we've put our hand to, and if in some way it could be realized, it would come very near immortality and be *second in point of unity*. Later, God willing, we'll describe a third best. But for the moment, what description should we give of this second-best state? What's the method by which a state like this is produced? (739a1–e7)[182]

The above translation of the italicized words is not the version usually accepted, as it states that the city is second 'in point of unity' (literally, 'as a one'), whereas most commentators read them as meaning second 'in point of

---

182. The text follows the translation by Saunders, 1970, but it is modified at 739e4–5, where the words italicized translate *kai hê mia deuterôs*.

merit'.[183] This text deserves to be studied with great care not only because of the corrections suggested but above all because it presents a good summary of the project of the *Laws*. Like the *Republic* and the *Statesman*, the *Laws* recognizes that perfect unity can never be achieved in a city. The two earlier dialogues did not actually state as much but tackled that difficulty by means which, although they made it possible to ascribe unity of a sort to the city (the unity of balance between the three kinds of soul and that of an interweaving of the warp and the woof into a single fabric), never allowed them to achieve perfect unity. However, as Aristotle complains,[184] the achievement of unity in the city constantly remains the ultimate purpose of its knowledgeable government and is always the objective of Platonic philosophy. We should make no mistake about it: the formulae that, in the *Laws*, allude to the *Republic* (such as the possession of all things in common under the government of one ruler, 739c) should remind us that in that dialogue the excellent constitution only achieved totally common ownership within one of the three groups of citizens (the guardians) and that the action of the statesman was really conceived to be in imitation of a divine and heavenly order. Thus Plato is suggesting not that the idea of perfection should be given up but, on the contrary, that one should always aspire to that excellence. Laws must remain committed to that (divine) unity of the city. They thus acquire both a function and a limit. Their function is definitely to promote the unity of the city, to make it 'one', knowing that this unity always at the same time means a *happy life* for the citizens. Their limit lies in their inability to realize that function throughout the 'whole city'.

183. The latter reading supports the idea that the *Laws* indicate that Plato abandoned the hope of governmental perfection and settled for second-best (legislation); cf. n. 165 above.

184. Aristotle regards the unity of the city as an irritating obsession of Plato's doctrine (*Politics*, II, 2).

That was the reservation that the *Statesman* had about them, but in the *Laws* the statesman does not play the same role. The *Statesman* required the law to preserve the city in the absence of a knowledgeable governor; the *Laws* expect it to construct that city, bringing about its unity.[185] Law is limited precisely in so far as it does not manage to unify *everything*, does not succeed in rendering 'all things' common. The unity of the future city will thus be less than total; it will be a second-grade unity. The shared function of those who are given specific jobs in the government of the city is to enable the law to determine as many things as possible in the city, or—to put it another way—to make it possible for intellect to set up the city. As we shall see, that constitution is an ongoing creation, which accommodates improvements and which expects cooperation from all the citizens.

In the course of nine of its twelve books, the *Laws* sets out the plan of the virtuous city, at every step of its foundation, and does so with remarkable precision. Moving on from the plans of Atlantis and the archaic Athens of the *Critias*,[186] Plato here constructs yet another descriptive fiction, using material with which the reader is particularly familiar since it is almost entirely Athenian. The legislative measures, magistracies and institutions of the *Laws* are all modelled on those of Athens.[187] The status and function of some of them are identical, but most are arranged differently and, in this Platonic city, play a role far removed from that which they played in Athens. The *Laws* describes the projected colony, setting out and redistributing the Athenian material in

185. So the law does not simply exist in the absence of a knowledgeable governor.
186. On the constitutional 'types' that archaic Athens and Atlantis represent, see Pradeau, 1997a, pp. 274–81.
187. To understand the details and see how the Platonic city borrows from Athens only the better to distinguish itself from it, see Morrow, 1993, or Gernet, 1951, pp. xcv–ccvi.

a foundation or *installation* (*oikêsis*) that begins with a description of the territory (in which the town is distinct from the outlying land), then moves on to the demography (specifying the origin and the number of its inhabitants), and finally describes the political regime, the details of which occupy the greater part of Books IV to XII.

Unlike Athens (which is an imperialistic maritime and commercial power), the city constructed in the *Laws* is a small, rural city, situated fifteen or so kilometres inland, isolated in a territory with no immediate neighbours (IV, 704a–705b). Its territory is fertile but not excessively so, providing both water and materials. So this can be a virtuous city (704d). This city is from the start regarded as a living entity,[188] and the conditions for its achieving excellence are that it be situated some way from the sea and not in possession of any excess of indispensable resources.

Those geographical and natural conditions are complemented by demographic ones: this living entity that is the city must not exceed a certain population, for should it do so its own land would not produce enough food to live on. That is why the number of citizens is limited to 5,040 households, that is to say 5,040 agricultural cultivators who, each with his own family, share the territory between them, dividing it into 5,040 equal allotments of land (V, 737c–738a). Almost all the citizens exercise the function of cultivators, but also that of fighters in the event of the city being at war.[189]

Apart from their common agricultural function, the citizens all, to a greater or lesser degree, participate in public

188. The idea has been established ever since the *Critias*, which describes cities as living beings. In the *Laws*, the same idea recurs as early as I, 636e, then again at III, 701–702.
189. This marks a significant break with the *Republic*: the city no longer has a separate warrior class. The requirement for the city to be united is better served by the warrior function being shared by all the citizens so that the city itself becomes a rampart (VI, 779b).

life, assuming certain tasks and magistracies and attending festivals. Plato no longer separates the citizens into different functional groups; but he does propose dividing them into four distinct census classes, based on how wealthy they are. However, a remarkable feature of this system is that certain limits are placed upon both wealth and poverty. The poorest citizen will never own less than one of the 5,040 plots of civic land and, with that same unit of land serving as the criterion for the distinctions between the four classes, the richest will never own more than four times the value of one plot (V, 744a–745a). A point that seldom attracts much attention is that this relatively restrained range of wealth is infinitely more restricted than that which existed in the Athenian democracy. Furthermore, in the city of the *Laws*, those limitations are strengthened by the ban placed on the possession of gold or silver by *any of the citizens*.[190] Scholars frequently point out that the *Laws* grant to every citizen a private property that the *Republic* denied to the guardians, and claim that this shows that the *Laws* is thereby bowing to a kind of pragmatic or even anthropological necessity. But what can private property amount to when financial wealth and commercial profit-making are ruled out and when, besides, that private property is inalienable because it constitutes one equal part (one 5,040th) of the public wealth?[191] In the *Republic*, the question of possessions was

190. The citizens are allowed only a currency, reserved for trading, which has no value outside the city. On this point, it is worth remembering that the *Republic* was content to forbid only the guardians the possession of gold and silver. The *Laws* definitively blocks the very possibility of enrichment for the entire population. See my study of the 'economy' of the *Laws*, Pradeau, 2000.
191. None of the citizens who own one of the 5,040 allotments are allowed to trade. Trading is a servile activity to be reserved for metics or foreigners (for whom permits of residence in the city territory are always of limited duration) and whose profits (the difference between what they are paid and their outlay) are to be fixed in advance by the guardians of the laws (XI, 919d–920c).

regulated and precisely determined only in the case of the guardians, the position of the other groups being left to the discretion of a limit probably imposed by the government (in accordance with the rules applying to the profession that they exercised). The situation is completely different in the *Laws*, where the 'allotments' possessed by all households are granted to them by a sovereign, foundational act in such a way that this distribution of property, which is a local distribution of the city territory, can never subsequently be overturned or called into question.[192] For a family group (a household grouped around a citizen), to own property is to be part of the city, to belong to it. There is no substitution for that participation nor can it ever be exchanged for anything, and the property itself, rather than being a free appropriation of a possession, designates the household as an indivisible and inalienable part of the city.[193] Thus, far from being a concession of autonomy to the family group, the property signifies its definitive membership of the community, the condition of which is that 'allotment'. For this, a part of the territory, is the principle upon which the rights of the family and their property are based. The elementary unit of the city, its smallest part, is not the citizen, not a human person, not the family, but the 1/5,040th part of the territory upon which the law confers perpetuity and indivisibility. This is the result of a political decision in consequence of which the family is constantly subordinated to the preser-

192. This is shown by the very strict laws relating to wills and, in general, to all transfers of property within a family (in cases of divorce or guardianship, for example). This collection of laws constitutes one of the longest and most detailed chapters of Platonic legislation, the purpose of which is crystal clear: the preservation (or transmission) of the 5,040 households must be faultless. As the Athenian says: 'neither you nor this property of yours belongs to yourselves, but to your clan, ancestors and descendants alike; and your clan and its property belong, even more absolutely, to the state' (XI, 923a6–b2; see this passage as a whole, XI, 922a–930e).
193. See VI, 772d–785b, and XI, 929e–930e.

vation of its allotment (and if that preservation demands it, the family has to be changed). It is also a determining demographic instrument since the population and the family group are governed in such a way as to preserve that political unit.[194] In the *Laws*, the family, a community created by birth, is first and foremost a community based on its allotted parcel of land within the territory of the city.[195]

The examples provided by property and by the family show that in the *Laws* Plato is bent on achieving the same ends as in the *Republic* but employs far more efficient means to do so. Instead of ruling out property and families (as in the case of the guardians), he transforms both in such a way that the community is made possible not by privation but by the activity of the citizens who, by cultivating their allotments and living off them, are constantly working to ensure the perpetuity of the city.

The families, thus distinguished by the particular portion of the territory that they are allotted to cultivate, live under a political regime with an institutional schema that must have been familiar to Greek readers. It was composed, according to the same pattern as that of the Athenian constitution, of magistracies (with military, judiciary or agrarian responsibilities), councils, and deliberative assemblies with more or less restricted membership. However, the familiarity of the schema and the positions of responsibility within it must soon have been dissipated by the overall organization that always puts the unity of the city first, together with the legal preservation of its initial form.

The three principal deliberative institutions of the city of

194. All this is clearly a far cry from the then current practices of Athens where, for example, a citizen was free to marry or not to marry, and could practise a private cult within a brotherhood, which is something prohibited in the city of the *Laws*, which permits only a public religion the true object of which is the city itself (X, 909d–910d).
195. Aristotle criticizes this, finding it absurd that a limit should be set on patrimonies rather than on the population. On Aristotle's critique of the *Laws*, see the important remarks of Bodéüs, 1985, pp. 367–72.

the *Laws* are assemblies (or councils), the number of whose members decreases as the importance of their decisions and power increases. First, there is an assembly in which all the citizens may participate (its functions are not specified); next a first council in which all four census classes take part by each electing ninety councillors, making a total of 360 (VI, 756b–e). These 360 elected men are divided into twelve groups of *prytaneis*. Each of these groups is responsible for organizing the affairs of the city for one month of the year (and deciding when to convene assemblies; VI, 758a–d).[196] Next up from this rotational council comes the 'nocturnal council', so called because it meets before dawn, so as to prepare for the day's orderly proceedings.[197] The task that falls to this council composed of 'guardians of the law', priests and specially chosen citizens, is the strange one of 'knowing': knowing what happens elsewhere, thanks to the reports of citizens sent out on missions to find out about other political regimes, knowing about their own constitution, in order to amend it if need be, and also resolving all difficulties of a legislative kind. The *Laws* sums up the work of these nocturnal councillors as follows: 'Their conference and discourse shall deal always with the subject of laws and of their own State' (XII, 951e5–7). The strange thing about these last pages of the *Laws* is their lack of precision as to the nature of the power of these nocturnal councillors despite the fact that they carry the greatest of responsibilities and only they, in the last analysis, can enable the city to achieve total virtue (XII, 962d). The only way to understand the status of this supreme council is by studying

196. The role of the assemblies, in particular that of the first 360 elected citizens, is defined only in a very allusive fashion. To sort out the details relating to magistracies and councils, see Gernet's rapid and clear introduction (1951), or the more precise chapter in Morrow 1993, pp. 155–78.
197. The 'Evening Council' would really be a better name for it, Brisson shows in his study on this institution (Brisson, 2001, pp. 161–77).

those who are its foremost members and who are also the most important figures in the city of the *Laws*: namely, 'the guardians of the laws'.

The thirty-seven citizen guardians of the laws chosen by the colonists who install themselves in the future city are to be its true founders (VI, 753a). For the first time in the dialogues, the founder of the city is also a citizen.[198] Here, the 'guardian' is no longer guarding a perfection of which he is not the author; instead, he himself fashions it, with the help of laws. The 'guardians of the laws' are at once the founders and the legislators of the city (so here again the law is defined as constitutive). In exercising this function they can draw upon the true understanding or correct opinion (I, 632c) upon which a knowledgeable exercise of power depends. As the *Statesman* stipulated, the power that they exercise will take the form of directing the choice and action of the other civic functions, the other magistracies. The magistracies, which are always distinguished by the public nature of their duties (the maintenance of order, the upkeep of the town and territory, education) are filled by election or by the drawing of lots, supervised by the thirty-seven guardians. The function of the latter is thus to preside over the attribution of magistracies, but also over respect for the laws and in particular the limitations imposed upon the acquisition of wealth (VI, 754d–755b). The guardians are not judges, and their function is not solely to apply the law. They may also modify it, adapt it, or even change it or introduce new legislation to cover a particular area. This remarkable recommendation (see VI, 769d–772d), which presupposes considerable reservations (there can be no question of modifying laws without prior research and consultation), is justified by the progressive nature of the constitution of the city, and the inevitable legislative work

198. By means of an intervention in the discussion, Plato takes the trouble to underline the fact that Clinias, one of the interlocutors, is to become one of the 'Guardians of the Laws' (VI, 753a).

[153]

of adaptation and correction. What Plato envisages is a progressive process of approximations (that will need to continue beyond the duration of a single magistracy and allow for those successively elected to correct and adjust as they go along) which will continue until such time as the institutions are functioning exactly as they should (VI, 772c).[199] This extended period is a very important one, for it encompasses the time of the actual foundation of the city of the *Laws*. Within it, between the moment when the thirty-seven guardians of the laws are chosen by the colonists and the moment when the entire creation comes to be definitively installed, by now provided with immutable laws, the city has been constructed and set in order by means of laws that are controlled by legislative bodies. The terrritory has been tamed, the town has been built and the citizens have been educated.[200] The political task has thus been completed and the thirty-seven guardians of the law now have only their function as founders to exercise. That is why, supplemented by other men chosen from amongst those whom the city has by now rendered virtuous, they proceed to change their status and become members of the 'nocturnal council'.

The nocturnal council is the result and predictable conclusion of the *Laws*. In view of the role that this dialogue ascribes to legislative constitution, it is to be expected that this role will come to an end once the institutions are installed in all their possible perfection. All that remains for the first city magistrates to do is to ensure that the institutions are respected and to maintain the constitutional

---

199. See also VI, 768c–e, where the Athenian explains that legislation is a perfectible task.
200. Among the magistracies of the *Laws*, Plato invents one surprising function, that of a kind of minister for the education of both girls and boys, who is responsible for schools and teaching. He says that 'of the highest offices of State, this is by far the most important' (VI, 765e; and see 764c–766d).

order. This is the role that falls to the Council, in which some of the guardians of the law are to be found, now joined by citizens distinguished by their virtue or their intelligence, one of whom is clearly the man who must be more interested in virtue and intelligence than anyone else: the man responsible for public education (XII, 960e–961c). The fact that young citizens do accede to intelligence and virtue proves that the city has achieved the goal for which it was conceived. It has come full circle; or rather, the living entity has been born. For with the nocturnal council, the city finds the soul that it previously lacked:

> *Athenian:* Well then, in the present circumstances, if our settlement of this territory is to be finished off properly, it looks as if we shall have to provide it with some constituent that understands (a) this target we have mentioned—the target, whatever we find it is, of the statesman, (b) how to hit it, and (c) which laws (above all) and which persons have helpful advice to give and which not. If a state lacks some such constituent, no one will be surprised to see it staggering from one irrational and senseless expedient to another in all its affairs.
>
> *Clinias:* That's true.
>
> *Athenian:* So is there any institution or constituent part of our state qualified and prepared to function as an organ of protection? Can we name one?
>
> *Clinias:* No, sir, not with much assurance, anyway. But if guess I must, I think your remarks point to the Council you said just now had to convene during the night.
>
> *Athenian:* You've caught my meaning splendidly, Clinias. As the drift of our present argument shows, that body must possess virtue in all its completeness . . . (XII, 962b4–d3)

So, since intellect and sensation are two species or functions of a soul, for its unity to be as perfect as possible, in imitation

[155]

of divine unity, the city must possess a soul.[201] The nocturnal council thus puts the finishing touch to the constitution, by making the life of the city subject to the intellect. This, along with the successful completion of the city of the *Laws*, rests upon the hypothesis that the city possesses a body sufficiently well ordered for the soul, unhampered, to be able to do what it does best, namely exercise its intellectual function. It is precisely the constitution of that body that is the subject of Book XII's city plan, which takes as its model the (divine) unity that it is possible for human beings to know, namely the unity of the world.

The order of the world

The city of the *Laws* is constructed in accordance with numbers and with movements. Right at the beginning of the plan of the city, the Athenian announces that 'every man who is making laws must understand at least this much — what number and what kind of number will be most useful for all States' (V, 737e7–738a2). There is, then, a political interest in number itself, quite apart from that which is numbered. Book VII of the *Republic* was already making that point when it ruled that the study of the mathematical sciences is an indispensable part of the education of future governors; and this was also suggested in the *Statesman* when it urged the statesman to master measurement (283b–287b). Here, however, measurement and number are, so to speak, represented figuratively, embodied in the plan of the city. So we can now work out how numbers can be used politically, and see what they can contribute to the city.

---

201. For Plato, the soul is the centre and subject of sensation. Sensation can only take place if information from the senses reaches the soul. On this subject, see the explanations of the *Timaeus*, 61c–69a. The third and last type or function of the soul is that which plays the vigorous part of a transmitter for that information (enabling reason to control desires). On the question of the soul in the *Laws*, see Saunders, 1962.

In the city, three kinds of things are measured and numbered: the territory; the assemblies and councils; and the movements of certain citizens. What is numbered with regard to the *circular* territory of the city is not its area (for that is limited by its resources),[202] but its division into a precise number of allotments, 5,040. As the Athenian explains, this number is chosen because it can be divided by the greatest number of divisors (V, 737e–738b), to which we may add that it is also the product of the multiplication of the seven prime numbers. He also explains that there are thus at least fifty-nine ways of dividing the city. The number 5,040 is thus chosen not only because it suits a city that is not to exceed 25,000 inhabitants, and not simply because it is a number that is easy to imagine, but above all, of course, because it tolerates so many divisions which represent possible ways of organizing and distributing the various elements of the city. Plato provides a number of examples, foremost among them the division of the whole town and the territory that surrounds it into twelve portions, each of which is placed under the protection of a god. He furthermore suggests that each household should be divided into two dwellings, one in one of the twelve urban areas, the other in one of the twelve rural ones (V, 745b–e).[203] This series of divisions, quite apart from their function of distributing religious ceremonies and rationalizing public life, plays two political roles. First, in imitation of what was probably Cleisthenes' great reform in Athens, it recomposes the tribal distribution of constitutional tasks.[204] Secondly, in

202. The territory must simply be large enough to feed the whole city.
203. On this subject, see Vidal-Naquet, 1986a.
204. Cleisthenes, at the very end of the fifth century, was the great Athenian reformer who, according to Herodotus and Aristotle, was the true creator of democracy. He is said to have altered the number of tribes by creating one hundred 'demes', grouped into thirty equal 'trittyes', themselves grouped into three to form ten tribes. On this reform and the various forms taken by the rationalization of the civic space, see Levêque and Vidal-Naquet, 1996.

a more strictly Platonic perspective, it allows each citizen to belong, in his own way, both to the rural and the urban parts of the city.[205] Through the household and the allotment which, as we have seen, is truly the inalienable (immortal) element in the city, Plato thus conceives of a way for the citizen, whoever he may be, to identify with one particular portion of the city. He may also be connected with that portion in a different way, through the assemblies or magistracies, either because he administers one or several portions of the territory or the town, as in the case of 'agronomes' and 'astynomes' (VI, 760a–764c),[206] or because he is one of the 360 members of the 1/14th of the city that sits in the first council.

Finally, numbers govern the movements of the citizens in so far as these affect the order of the city. As the *Laws* constantly reminds us, thanks to its physical material, the city is a reality in movement. As Critias suggested, it is therefore important to coordinate all its different movements. This is facilitated by the circular form of the city, for this makes it possible to relate movements of varying speeds to one another by turning them into concentric movements (at the same time installing the sacred portion of the city at its centre, which is reserved for the gods and their altars). This is what the legislators aim to achieve by arranging for the citizens to rotate. The agronomes and the craftsmen thus move from section to section according to a precise calendar, and the ordinary inhabitants move to and fro between their two dwellings. Contrary to the proverb ('a man with two

205. Clearly thereby preventing the development of an agrarian and an urban party. Cleisthenes' reform, although less radical, was designed to have a similar effect, since each 'trittys' brought together ten town 'demes': ten demes of the inland territory and ten of the coastal area.

206. For example, each of the twelve sections recruits five agronomes, each of which then selects twelve young apprentices to assist him. In the course of a year, each group studies the twelve sections of the territory, in order to get to know it (and so that the best of them may then be chosen as guardians of the territory).

houses loses his mind'), this combination of circular movements and toing and froing between the town and the countryside ought to get all the citizens to take an interest in the entire city territory, thereby doing away with the opposition between town and country that bedevilled Athens.

As can be seen, the use of numbers affords every citizen a chance to get his own activities (and movements) to fit in with the city and also with the other parts of the particular section in which his activity may engage him. The function of numbers is to limit and set in order terms that are indefinite and hard to control (human patterns of behaviour as well as the area and aspect of the territory). Numbering constitutes the instrument by which change can be made orderly. In this respect, it serves the same function as the law, and that is why the city's constitutive legislation relies on it as an aid. Laying down general prescriptions at the expense of the individual is not what legislation means. Rather, it finds ways of setting single and multiple elements in order together: that is why to legislate is to count.[207]

The organization of the city, in which geometry and arithmetic are employed to construct a regular order and to impart stability to the movements of a shifting material, is inspired by that which presides over the arrangement of the universe, as is described in the *Timaeus*. For the craftsmen who fashion the city, the model is the god who fashioned the world: political demiurgy imitates the cosmological demiurgy and their products are similar. In its own way, the circular city of the *Laws* is an image of the world's sphere. The former reproduces a finite material, contained and ordered within the limits of a circular form and circular movements. And there are other similarities, the most striking of which involves numbering: for instance, combinations of divisions of the number 5,040 call to mind the way in which the demiurge in the *Timaeus* constructs the body of the world. Similarly, just as four elements combine to form the world

207. See V, 737e f., and VI, 757a f.

[159]

(linked by proportional relations that make it possible for them to form a unit, 31b–32c), so too the city of the *Laws* is composed of four classes of citizens (the value of a single allotment is what makes it possible to establish proportional relations between their respective riches, if not between one another personally).

Finally, in imitation of the living entity that is the world, the political living entity aspires to a self-sufficiency and an equilibrium that it strives to achieve by endowing the movements of its parts with such perfection as can be theirs. What we have here is the political physiology that the *Critias* was the first to test out: the political fiction of the *Laws* adopts the schema (and eventually the argument) of the creation of the world by a craftsman god. The interest of this cosmological fiction lies in its ability to identify and distinguish clearly between the elements and forces that combine to bring the world into existence: a divine reason or intellect works to control recalcitrant necessity in order to bestow the most perfect order possible upon the basic material. Political demiurgy plays a similar role, for it too, in its turn, conceives of a fabrication produced by reason and accompanied by certain conditions which, as the interlocutors of the *Laws* recognize, may never all be achieved at once.

The epistemological status of understanding of the city presented here is thus akin to that of the cosmology of the *Timaeus*: this knowledge proposes a rational fictional model for the reality that it aims to explain, a model based upon a limited number of axioms.[208] All this is laid out very clearly in Book X of the *Laws*, which is, without doubt, as G. Naddaf puts it, the dialogue's 'corner stone'.[209] The

208. See Brisson's indispensable introduction to his translation of the *Timaeus*, 2000b, p. 13f.
209. The existence of the gods and the understanding of this that the immortal and intelligent soul may gain constitute the double condition for the overall system of the *Laws*. See Naddaf, 1992, p. 446 and the whole of Chapter VII.

[160]

constitution founded by discourse in the *Laws* must *conform to nature*, that is to say, as Plato himself understands it, it must conform to 'that which is the first cause of becoming and perishing in all things', namely, the soul (X, 891e5–6). To found the city, its constitution and its legislation *in conformity with nature* presupposes that the intelligent order of the city is also that of nature, as presented by a cosmology. This is what is established in the passage devoted to the existence of the gods in the essential portion of Book X. Plato's demonstration, unique of its kind,[210] is cosmological. This can come as no surprise to readers of the *Timaeus*, and it means that the *Laws* shares with the *Timaeus* (and with the *Critias*) the same understanding of the world as a living totality endowed with both a soul and a body. The Athenian thus echoes Timaeus when he declares that the soul precedes the body as the cause of movement (in particular at 893a). The *Laws* retains only the main features of the cosmology of the *Timaeus*: the four elements that constitute the body of the world (891c), the fact that it belongs to the physical order of generation and corruption (891e), the mutual transformation of the elements and parts of the world (893b–894a) that are all caught up in an overall movement the true cause of which is the self-moving soul (894–895b). The order of the world, of which Timaeus offered a representation, can be explained on the basis of dynamic hypotheses: both 'becoming', whatever the forms of generation and corruption, and also 'thought' are kinds of movement.[211] The *Laws* stresses this, insisting on the nature of the soul, which is the principle behind the ten different kinds of movements (895b3–4). It is this cosmological

210. See Naddaf, 1992, p. 439, and also Brisson, 1995.
211. The main hypotheses of Platonic 'physics' relate to the elemental (and geometric) constitution of bodies, their movements and their resulting relative positioning. They are therefore set out in the *Timaeus*. For an explanation, see Brisson, 1998b; also O'Brien, 1984. Finally, I myself have studied the local aspect to his 'physics' in Pradeau, 1995.

primacy that needs to be underlined to counter 'atheistic' physiologists and in support of the primacy of the divine. We have thus come full circle, for the cosmo(theo)logical message (the world is intelligently ordered) connects with the cognitive (or epistemological) message (the world can be understood by the intellect). A political constitution can aspire to excellence if it models itself upon the thought (and circular movement) of the intellect of the world. That is why it must be arranged and organized in accordance with the best kind of (circular) movement, and thus itself come to resemble the divine (the '*homoiôsis theô*')[212] that the *Alcibiades* urges man to strive for. It is also why an eminently high political status is ascribed to astronomy, the area of knowledge which, as was suggested already in the *Republic*,[213] makes it possible to associate human understanding (in its most elevated hypothetical and discursive form), the government of the city and the order of the world. It is via the astronomical order that political demiurgy can make itself resemble the cosmic demiurgy; and, as Plato has been indicating, in a programmatic fashion at least, ever since the *Gorgias*,[214] this presupposes that the specific kind of knowledge required for the political technique is an understanding of nature (the nature of the world).

But a particular feature of the political fiction constituted by the city is that it represents a kind of knowledge that can create and produce, intervening in the generation of its object; politics is a technique. That is why, in the last analysis, its status is not identical to that of cosmology, which serves as a precedent or support for it, rather than simply as a model; for, as Critias said in the introduction to his unfinished story:

---

212. On this 'assimilation to god', the future influence of which was to be considerable, particularly on middle and neo-Platonism, see the *Theaetetus*, 176b f., the *Republic*, VI, 500a and X, 613a, and the *Laws*, IV, 716a–b.
213. IX, 592a–b.
214. 507e–508a.

It is easier, Timaeus, for someone to give the impression
that he is a successful speaker when he speaks of gods to
an audience of mortals. The audience's lack of experience
and sheer ignorance concerning a subject they can never
know for certain provide the would-be speaker with great
eloquence. (*Critias*, 107a7–b4).

The *Laws* adds that, even if the city that it constructs is a
fiction, it is nevertheless designed for a political use, that is
to say in a process that involves a physical transformation of
reality.[215] In the end, we see that cosmology is a far more
approximate kind of knowledge than politics, since, whereas
the former can be content with a plausible representation,
the latter must provide an understanding of its object
sufficient to lead to its transformation.

The city must be genuinely understood if it is to be
transformed in reality. This philosophical requisite is
repeated in every dialogue, but in the *Laws* it becomes the
very principle of government. For, through its nocturnal
council, the city now itself becomes the author of its own
transformation. If the city itself aims to assume the function
of knowledgeable government, it must manifest an intellect
that can govern. Something within it must think. The *raison
d'être* of the nocturnal council, the 'intellect that governs'
(XII, 961e) is, of course, to direct the whole living entity
which, without that organ, would be bereft of both sensation
and intelligence (962c).[216] But why does this intellect arrive
upon the scene so late, seemingly right at the end of the
operation?[217] Why does it not intervene earlier, as in the

215. The *Critias* provides a critique of politics, whereas the *Laws* defines a
plausible constitution and plausible legislation that can actually be set up.
216. See Saunders, 1962.
217. As Neschke pointed out to me, this question does not arise if one
accepts that the intellect is always already present, in the form of the order
created by the legislator: intellect *is* the law.

cosmological explanation or even in the genesis of a human being, where it brings to an end an initial period of turmoil by imposing regular movements upon its material? The reason is that, as in a human body, the intellect, the highest function of the soul, can only operate once a certain order exists and the soul is no longer caught up in the turmoil of physical agitation (as is the case in the early infancy of a human being, when the child needs time to learn to control the movements of its body).[218] It is therefore necessary for the body and the soul of any living entity to be linked together in such a way that the soul envelops the movements of the body; only then will the soul be able to exercise its intellectual function. Clearly, the nocturnal council can only sit once the city has been organized in such a way that the double function of its soul—understanding and movement —can be exercised.[219] The council will assume its duties at such time as the city is rotating with the regularity that has been introduced by its laws. The correlation of that regularity is the citizens' education and an 'altogether clear' explanation of the purpose of legislation (964c). A pro-gramme of persuasion (which falls to the preambles that precede the laws) and explanation, an educational pro-gramme, is therefore indispensable. Only when it is completed can certain guardians of the laws at last set about guiding and advising the city, thereby allowing it the possibility of attaining to total virtue.

Once provided with this intellect, the city recovers the organizing principle that set in order all that exists beneath the heavens (967b). It comes as no surprise to find that in the *Laws* the city has become the active author of its own transformation, possessed of understanding (it has both a

218. See the explanation offered by the *Timaeus*, 42e–44b, which contains exactly the same remarks on the state of a living entity that is not controlled by the soul as those of the last pages of the *Laws*.
219. As we are reminded by a last remark in the final description of the nocturnal council (XII, 966c–968a).

soul and an intellect), and also the creator of its own movement (itself immobile, it rotates on its axis). Understanding and controlling itself, it achieves what Plato's dialogues have required of individual human beings if they are to fulfill their natural potential. The city uses its intellect to understand the intelligible principle of the order of the world and uses this as the norm for its own behaviour: the city philosophizes.

Rather than define human affairs as the things, people, objects, and activities that exist within the limits instituted by the city, Plato chooses to gather them all together and organize them within a single system (*sustêma*). The *Laws* describes the order and conditions of this system. Far from representing a step backward, a defeated or exasperated return to the constraints of 'reality', Plato's last text manifests a truly foundational political and philosophical ambition: to extend power, philosophically conceived, to all the objects of the city, to all human affairs. From an epistemological point of view, the ambitions of Plato's political science have thus been growing ever since the *Statesman* and in the *Laws* achieve, not a system of types of understanding, but a system of reality. The reason why this system is deployed as a *politeia* is that the city is the sole domain and, in the last analysis, the sole subject of human excellence. It is because this excellence consists in an understanding of what *is* that the city presupposes an enquiry into nature, to be carried out by someone who knows things as they are, that is to say a philosopher. The city is not a natural state of affairs, nor is it either a herd or even a family. It is a 'constitutional' order produced by intelligent research into what is most suitable for beings living a communal life together. In his plan for a system of intelligible reality and unprecedented rationality, Plato chose not to pursue the project of a trilogy (*Timaeus*, *Critias*, *Hermocrates*) that would have separated the world, man and the city into three distinct dialogues or accounts. Instead, he decided to realize his plan by means of a single

[165]

description of the city as the only place of truth, and hence also the goal of his philosophical doctrine. The *Laws* constitute the first systematic philosophy of the city.

Conclusion

In Plato's dialogues, the object of politics is the city and its goal is the city's unity. Not one of these texts ever rejects that plan, the concept of which is truly philosophical since it presupposes an enquiry *into nature*, an enquiry that can only be carried out by a man who understands things as they are, that is to say a philosopher. In making the city a physical living entity, Plato opted to set his political analysis within the framework of a physiological (or physical) programme of research in which he linked together two things that his successors (Aristotle first and foremost) would hasten to draw apart: an understanding of nature and an understanding of political affairs. Yet there is no reason why political science should not study the nature of the city and what is best for it. Political physiology thus conceived is not the kind of political naturalism that Plato opposed when he showed that a political community could not be seen simply as a gathering of people, certain of whom would assume command. A city is not a natural state of affairs, not a herd nor even a family: it is the 'constitutional' order produced by intelligent research into what is best for beings living a communal life together. It is against the yardstick of this definition and with the idea that political unity will never be a given factor but always something to be created that Plato judged and condemned as failures all known forms of political groupings. However, Plato's political thought likewise opposes the view that a city, because it gathers people together and some kind of power has to be wielded amongst them, is a place where thought and morality should give way in the face of the need to impose order and govern. That hypothesis, which also assumes that humankind is naturally weak and irremediable, is certainly not Platonic. The imperfection of human nature will never stop people from conceiving of a better common order than that which rules their life, nor will it prevent them from understanding that it is thanks to thought that they can hope to approach it.

The Neoplatonic movement of the third to the fifth centuries AD certainly strove to restore the unity of the Platonic world, but did so from a theological point of view alien to the dialogues and hostile to their political struggle. Plato's project of a *system* of philosophy, a system based on the combination of intelligible reality and total rationality, was not to find an echo until the modern (rationalist) age. The kinship that may thus be detected between a political treatise by Hobbes or Spinoza and a dialogue by Plato is not merely that which links together the works of a common tradition of 'political philosophy'. Rather, and far more fundamentally, it is that which associates works which have a systematic conceptual framework, which opt not to relegate the political question to the world of possibility and approximation, but to make the political community the sole place for truths and human perfection, so that, in the last analysis, it becomes the ultimate goal of philosophical doctrine. In this sense, both those modern works and Plato's are philosophies of the city.

Bibliography

This bibliography brings together the studies listed in the book and, in addition, other key relevant works of Platonic scholarship. It may be complemented by reference to the 'Bibliographie platonicienne', published every five years in the journal *Lustrum*, by H. Cherniss (*Lustrum*, 4 and 5, 1959 and 1960) and, from 1977, by L. Brisson (*Lustrum*, 20, 25, 26, 30 and 34); the latest instalment (1990–1995) has been published by Vrin, 1999.

All works are referred to in full in the Bibliography and in short form (author, date, page ref.) elsewhere in the book.

Annas, J., 'Plato', in *Greek Thought. A Guide to Classical Knowledge*, J. Brunschwig and G.E.R. Lloyd (eds), translated by C. Porter, Cambridge, Mass./London, Harvard University Press, 2000, pp. 672–92.

Annas, J. and C. Rowe (eds), *Perspectives on Plato, Modern and Ancient*, Cambridge, Mass., Harvard University Press, forthcoming.

Badiou, A., 'L'Outrepassement politique du philosophe de la communauté', in *Politique et modernité*, Paris, Osiris, 1992, pp. 55–67.

Baltes, M., 'Plato's School, the Academy', in *Hermathena*, University of Dublin, 155, 1993, pp. 5–26.

Bambrough, J.R. (ed.), *Plato, Popper and Politics*, Cambridge, Heffer, 1967.

Benson, H.H., *Socratic Wisdom: the Model of Knowledge in Plato's Early Dialogues*, Oxford, Oxford University Press, 2000.

Bertrand, J.-M., *De l'écriture à l'oralité. Lecture des* Lois *de Platon*, Paris, Publications de la Sorbonne, 1999.

Bizos, M., *Lysias: Discours II*, edition and translation, Paris, Belles Lettres, 1926.

Bobonich, C., 'Persuasion, Compulsion, and Freedom in Plato's *Laws*', in *Classical Quarterly*, 41, 1991, pp. 365–88.

Bodéüs, R., 'Pourquoi Platon a-t-il compose les *Lois*?', in *Les Etudes Classiques*, 53, 1985, pp. 367–72.

Bordes, J., *Politeia dans la pensée grecque jusqu'à Aristote*, Paris, Belles Lettres, 1982.

Brisson, L., 'De la philosophie politique à l'épopée, le *Critias* de Platon', in *Revue de métaphysique et de morale*, 75, 1970, pp. 402–38.

Brisson, L., 'Les listes des vertus sans le *Protagoras* et dans la *République*', in P. Demont (ed.), *Problèmes de la morale antique*, Amiens, Faculté des Lettres d'Amiens, 1993, pp. 75–92.

Brisson, L., 'Une comparaison entre le livre X des *Lois* et le *Timée*', in *Le temps philosophique* (Université de Paris-X Nanterre), 1, 1995, pp. 115–30.

Brisson, L., 'La notion de *phthonos* chez Platon', in *Recherches sur la philosophie et le langage*, 18, 1996, pp. 41–59.

Brisson, L. and M. Canto-Sperber, 'Zur socialen Gliederung der Polis (Buch II, 372d-IV, 427c)', in O. Hoffe (ed.), *Platon, Politeia*, Berlin, Akademie Verlag, 1997, pp. 95–117.

Brisson, L., *Plato the Myth Maker*, translated by G. Naddaf, Chicago/London, University of Chicago Press, 1998a.

Brisson, L., *Le Même et l'Autre dans la structure ontologique du Timée de Platon*, Sankt Augustin, Academia, 1998[3]b.

Brisson, L., 'Interprétation du mythe du *Politique*', in *Lectures de Platon*, Paris, Vrin, 2000a, pp. 169–205.

Brisson, L., *Platon: Timée-Critias*, Paris, Flammarion, 2000[4]b.

Brisson, L., 'Le Collège de veille (*nukterinòs súllogos*)', in F.L. Lisi (ed.), *Plato's* Laws *and its historical significance. Selected Papers of the 1*[st] *International Congress of Ancient thought, Salamanca, 1998*, Sankt Augustin, Academia, 2001, pp. 161–77.

Brunschwig J., 'Platon. La *République*', in F. Chatelet, O. Duhamel and E. Pisier (eds), *Dictionnaire des œuvres politiques*, Paris, PUF, 1986, pp. 638–52.

Burnyeat, M.F., 'Sphinx Without a Secret', in *New York Review of Books*, 30 May and 10 October 1985.

Cambiano, G., *Platone e le tecniche*, Rome/Bari, Laterza, 1991².

Cherniss, H., 'The relation of the *Timaeus* to Plato's later dialogues', in R.E. Allen (ed.), *Studies in Plato's Metaphysics*, London, Routledge and Kegan Paul, 1965, pp. 339–78.

Cooper, J.M., (ed.), *Plato: Complete Works with Introduction and Notes*, Indianapolis/Cambridge, Hackett, 1997.

Dixsaut, M., 'Une politique vraiment conforme à la nature', in C.J. Rowe (ed.), *Reading the* Statesman. *Proceedings of the III Symposium Platonicum*, Sankt Augustin, Academia, 1995, pp. 253–273.

Dodds, E.R., *Plato, Gorgias*, Oxford, Clarendon Press, 1959.

Dombrowski, D.A., *Plato's Philosophy of History*, Washington, University Press of America, 1981.

Ferrari, G.R.F., 'Strauss's Plato', in *Arion*, 5.2 (1997), pp. 36–65.

Festugière, A.J., *Commentary on the* Timaeus, 5 vols, Paris, Vrin, 1966–68.

Finley M.I., *Democracy Ancient and Modern*, London, Chatto and Windus, 1973.

Gernet, L., Introduction to the *Laws*, Paris, Belles Lettres, 1951, vol. 1, pp. xciv–ccvi.

Gill C., 'The Origin of the Atlantis Myth', in *Trivium*, 11, 1976, pp. 1–11.

Gill C., 'The Genre of the Atlantis Story', in *Classical Philology*, 72, 1977, pp. 287–304.

Gill C., 'Plato and Politics, the *Critias* and the *Politicus*', in *Phronesis*, 24, 1979, pp. 148–67.

Gill, C., *Plato: Timaeus 17–27 and Critias*, introduction and translation, Bristol, Bristol Classical Press, 1980.

Gill, C., 'Rethinking Constitutionalism in the *Statesman* 291–303', in C.J. Rowe (ed.), *Reading the* Statesman. *Proceedings of the III Symposium Platonicum*, Sankt Augustin, Academia, 1995, pp. 292–305.

Gill, C., 'Protreptic and Dialectic in Plato's *Euthydemus*', in T.M. Robinson and L. Brisson (eds), *Plato: Euthydemus, Lysis, Charmides: Proceedings of the V Symposium Platonicum, Selected Papers*, Sankt Augustin, Academia, 2000, pp. 133–43.

Guthrie, W.K.C., *A History of Greek Philosophy*, Cambridge, Cambridge University Press, 1969, vol. 3.

Hansen, M.H., *The Athenian Democracy in the Age of Demosthenes. Structures, Principles and Ideology*, translated by J.A. Crook, Oxford, Blackwell, 1991.

Hanson, V.D., *The Western Way of War, Infantry Battle in Classical Greece*, Berkeley, University of California Press, 2000[2].

Hegel, G.W.F., *Reason in History*, translated by R.S. Hartmann, Library of Liberal Arts, Bobbs-Merrill, Indianapolis, 1953.

Jacoby, F., *Atthis. The Local Chronicles of Ancient Athens*, Oxford, Clarendon Press, 1949.

Joly, H., *Le renversement platonicien: Logos, Episteme, Polis*, Paris, Vrin, 1985[2].

Kahn, C.H., 'Plato's Funeral Oration: the Motive of the *Menexenus*', in *Classical Philology*, vol. LVIII, 4, 1963, pp. 220–34.

Kahn, C.H., 'Drama and Dialectic in Plato's *Gorgias*', in *Oxford Studies in Ancient Philosophy*, 1, 1983, pp. 75–121.

Kahn, C.H., *Plato and the Socratic Dialogue: the Philosophical Use of a Literary Form*, Cambridge, Cambridge University Press, 1996.

Kerferd, G., *The Sophistic Movement*, Cambridge, Cambridge University Press, 1981.

Klosko, G., *Plato's Political Theory*, New York/London, Methuen, 1986.

Lane, M., 'A New Angle on Utopia: the Political Theory of the *Politicus*', in C.J. Rowe (ed.), *Reading the Statesman. Proceedings of the III Symposium Platonicum*, Sankt Augustin, Academia, 1995, pp. 276–91.

Lane, M., *Method and Politics in Plato's Statesman*, Cambridge, Cambridge University Press, 1998.

Levêque, P. and P. Vidal-Naquet, *Cleisthenes the Athenian*, translated by D. Ames, Atlantic Highlands, New Jersey, Humanities Press, 1996.

Lisi, F.L., *Einheit und Vielheit des platonischen Nomosbegriffes: eine Untersuchung zur Beziehung von Philosophie und Politik bei Platon*, Königstein/Ts., A. Hain, 1985.

Lisi, F.L., Introduction to Spanish translation of *Platon: Leyes*, Madrid, Gredos, 2 vols, 1999.

Lisi, F.L., 'Les fondements métaphysiques du *nomos* dans les *Lois*', in *Revue philosophique*, 190, 2000, pp. 57–82.

Loraux, N., *The Invention of Athens*, translated by A. Sheridan, Cambridge, Mass./London, Harvard University Press, 1986.

Loraux, N., *L'invention d'Athènes. Histoire de l'oraison funèbre dans la 'cité classique'*, Paris, Payot, 1993[2].

Matthews, G., *Socratic Perplexity and the Nature of Philosophy*, Oxford, Oxford University Press, 1999.

Morrow, G.R., *Plato's Cretan City, A Historical Interpretation of the Laws*, Princeton, Princeton University Press, 1993[2].

Mossé, C., *Politique et société en Grèce ancienne. Le modèle athénien*, Paris, Aubier, 1995.

Naddaf, G., *L'origine et l'évolution du concept grec de phusis*, Leweston/Queenstown/Lampeter, E. Mellen Press, 1992.

Neschke, A. (A.B. Hentschke–Neschke), *Politik und Philosophie bei Plato und Aristoteles. Die Stellung der Nomoi im platonischen Gesamtwerk und die politische Theorie des Aristoteles*, Frankfurt-am-Main, Klostermann, 1971.

Neschke, A., *Platonisme politique et théorie du droit naturel*, vol. 1, Louvain, Bibliothèque philosophique de Louvain, 1995.

O'Brien, D., *Theories of Weight in the Ancient World*, vol. II, *Plato, Weight and Sensation*, Paris/Leiden, Belles Lettres/E. Brill, 1984.

Owen, G.E.L., 'The Place of the *Timaeus* in Plato's Dialogues' (1953), in R.E. Allen (ed.), *Studies in Plato's Metaphysics*, London, Routledge and Kegan Paul, 1965, pp. 313–38.

Pappas, N., *Plato and the Republic*, London, Routledge, 1995.

Penner, T., 'Socrates and the Early Dialogues', in H. Krant (ed.), *The Cambridge Companion to Plato*, Cambridge, Cambridge University Press, 1992, pp. 121–69.

Piérart, M., *Les Lois. Platon et la cité grecque. Théorie et réalité dans la constitution des Lois*, Brussels, Académie Royale de Belgique, 1974.

Popper, K., *The Open Society and its Enemies*, vol. 1, London, Routledge and Kegan Paul, 1945.

Pradeau, J.-F., 'Être quelque part, occuper une place. *Topos* et *Khôra* dans le *Timée*', in *Les Études Philosophiques*, 3, 1995, pp. 275–299.

Pradeau, J.-F., *Le monde de la politique. Sur le récit atlante de Platon, Timée (17–27) et Critias*, Sankt Augustin, Academia, 1997a.

Pradeau, J.-F., *Platon: Ménexène*, translated by L. Méridier,

Introduction and notes by J.-F. Pradeau, Paris, Belles Lettres, 1997b.

Pradeau, J.-F., *Platon, Critias*, translation and commentary, Paris, Belles Lettres, 1997c.

Pradeau, J.-F., *Platon et la Cité*, Paris, Presses universitaires de France, 1997d.

Pradeau, J.-F., *Platon, Gorgias*, translation by A. Croiset, introduction and notes by J.-F. Pradeau, Paris, Belles Lettres, 1997e.

Pradeau, J.-F., 'L'âme et la moelle. Les conditions psychiques et physiologiques de l'anthropologie dans le *Timée* de Platon', in *Archives de philosophie*, 61, 1998, pp. 489–518.

Pradeau, J.-F., *Platon*, Paris, Ellipses, 1999.

Pradeau, J.-F., 'Sur les *lots* de la cité de *Lois*. Remarques sur l'institution des *kleroi*, *Cahiers Glotz*, XI, 2000, pp. 25–36.

Pradeau, J.-F., *Platon, Alcibiades*, translation by C. Marbœuf and J.-F. Pradeau, introduction and notes by J.-F. Pradeau, Paris, Flammarion, GF, 2002[2].

Robin, L., 'Platon et la science sociale', in *Revue de métaphysique et de morale*, XX, 1913, pp. 211–15 (reprinted in Robin L. *La pensée hellénique des origines à Epicure*, Paris, PUF, 1941).

Rowe, C.J. (ed.), *Reading the* Statesman. *Proceedings of the III Symposium Platonicum*, Sankt Augustin, Academia, 1995a.

Rowe, C.J., *Plato: Statesman*, translation and commentary, Warminster, Aris & Phillips, 1995b.

Rowe, C., 'Socrates' and 'The *Politicus* and Other Dialogues' in C. Rowe and M. Schofield (eds), *The Cambridge History of Greek and Roman Political Thought*, Cambridge, Cambridge University Press, 2000, pp. 164–89, 233–57.

Samaras, A., *Plato on Democracy*, Bern, Peter Lang, 2002.

Saunders, T.J., 'The structure of the Soul and the State in Plato's *Laws*', in *Eranos*, 60, 1962, pp. 37–55.

Saunders, T.J., *Plato: The Laws*, translation and introduction, Harmondsworth, Penguin Classics, 1970.

Saunders, T.J., *Plato's Penal Code. Tradition, Controversy and Reform in Greek Penology*, Oxford, Clarendon Press, 1991.

Sayers, S., *Plato's Republic: An Introduction*, Edinburgh, Edinburgh University Press, 1999.

Schmid, W.T., *On Manly Courage: a Study of Plato's Laches*, Carbondale/Edwardsville, Southern Illinois University Press, 1992.

Schofield, M., 'Approaching the *Republic*' and 'Plato and Practical Politics' in C. Rowe and M. Schofield (eds), *The Cambridge History of Greek and Roman Political Thought*, Cambridge, Cambridge University Press, 2000, pp. 190–257, 293–302.

Schöpsdau, K., Translation and commentary of Plato's *Laws* (I–III), *Platon: Nomoi* I-III *(Gesetze); Übersetzung und Kommentar*, Göttingen, Vandenhoeck & Ruprecht, 1994.

Smith, A., *The Theory of Moral Sentiments*, 1790[6], Oxford, Oxford University Press, 1976.

Stalley, R., *An Introduction to Plato's Laws*, Oxford, Blackwell, 1983.

Strauss, L., *The City and Man*, Chicago, University of Chicago Press, 1964.

Vegetti, M. and M. Abbate (eds), *La Repubblica di Platone nella tradizione antica*, Napoli, 1999.

Vernant, J.-P., *Myth and Society in Ancient Greece*, translated by Janet Lloyd, New York, Zone Books, 1988.

Vidal-Naquet P., 'Hérodote et l'Atlantide: entre les Grecs et les Juifs. Réflexion sur l'historiographie du siècle des lumières', in *Quaderni di Storia*, 16, July-December 1982, pp. 3–76.

Vidal-Naquet, P., 'A Study in Ambiguity: Artisans in the Platonic city', in *The Black Hunter*, translated by A. Szegedy-Maszak, Baltimore/London, The Johns Hopkins University Press, 1986a, pp. 224–48.

Vidal-Naquet, P., 'Athens and Atlantis: Structure and Meaning of a Platonic Myth', in *The Black Hunter*, translated by A. Szegedy-Maszak, Baltimore/London, The Johns Hopkins University Press, 1986b, pp. 263–84.

Vidal-Naquet P., 'L'atlantide et les nations', in *Représentations de l'origine. Littérature, histoire, civilisation*, Cahiers CRLH-CIRAOI, 4, 1987, Université de la Réunion (reprinted in *La démocratie grecque vue d'ailleurs*, Paris, Flammarion, 1990, pp. 139–159).

Vlastos, G., 'Isonomia', in *American Journal of Philology*, 64, 1953, pp. 337–66 (reprinted in *Platonic Studies*, Princeton 1981[2], pp. 164–203).

Vlastos, G., *Socrates, Ironist and Moral Philosopher*, Cambridge, Cambridge University Press, 1991.

Vlastos, G., M.F. Burnyeat (ed.), *Socratic Studies*, Cambridge, Cambridge University Press, 1994.

Index

Annas, Julia, 136n.165
Aristophanes, 52n.71
Aristotle, 36, 57, 60,
    100n.119, 101n.122,
    138n.169, 146n.184,
    151n.195

Badiou, Alain, 2n.1
Baltes, Matthias, 2n.2
Bertrand, Jean-Marie,
    101n.121–22, 103n.124,
    107–8
Bizos, Marcel, 27n.32
Bobonich, Christopher,
    137n.167, 142n.177
Bodéus, Richard, 151n.195
Brisson, Luc, 11n.8, 32n.40,
    47n.63, 79n.100,
    116n.141, 152n.197,
    160n.208, 161n.210,
    161n.211
Brunschwig, Jacques, 45n.60,
    49

Cambiano, Giuseppe, 84n.107
Cherniss, Harold F.,
    135n.161

citizen, citizenship, 45–48,
    60, 65, 94, 127,
    148–51

democracy, 3–4, 9, 13n.11,
    35n.46
dialectics, 66
Dionysius of Halicarnassus,
    16n.15
Dixsaut, Monique, 90
Dodds, Eric D., 38n.52
dunamis (power, faculty), 63

êthos (way of life, acquired
    characteristic), 100–12

family, 48n.66, 149–51
forms (ideas, intelligible
    realities), 46n.61, 64

Gernet, Louis, 134n.160,
    147n.187, 152n.196
Gill, Christopher, 56n.77, 96,
    135n.161, 136n.163
gods, divinity, 68, 118, 162

Hanson, Victor D., 47n.63

Hegel, 61n.81
Herodotus, 20n.24, 21n.27

isonomia (equality in law),
    30–31

justice, 44, 62, 76, 92

Kahn, Charles, H. 7n.4,
    38n.52, 56n.77
kairos (opportunity), 90
khrêsis (use, utility), 77,
    81–82, 112
Klosko, Georges, 136n.165
kosmos (world), 115, 156,
    160–65

Lane, Melissa, 85n.108
law, 95–109, 118n.146,
    142–43, 159
Lisi, Francisco L.,
    107n.131–32, 109n.136
Loraux, Nicole, 14, 17,
    22n.28, 23
Lysias, 27–28, 35
Lysias (Pseudo), 16–22

mimêsis (imitation), 103–4
Morrow, Glenn R., 134n.160,
    147n.187, 152n.196
Mossé, Claude, 65n.87
myth, 61, 79

Naddaf, Gérard, 116n.140,
    136n.165, 160,
    161n.210
Neschke, Ada B., 134n.159,
    135n.162, 142n.177

O'Brien, Denis, 161n.211

opinion, belief (*doxa*), 61–62,
    64, 92, 153
Owen, Guilym E.L., 135n.161

paradigm, 79
philosophy 52–53, 55–56,
    79–80, 84
Piérart, Marcel, 134n.159,
    136n.165
Plato
  —*Alcibiades*
    130c3: 44n.59
    133d–134e: 12n.10
  —*Apology*
    24b9: 12
    26b5: 12
    31d: 9
    31e–32a: 10
  —*Charmides*
    160b–d: 92n.114
  —*Cratylus*
    388b–390d: 81
  —*Critias*
    107a7–b4: 162–63
    109c10–11: 131
    111e: 130
    112d–e: 131
    113d–e: 128
    115c–d: 128
    118a–119a: 129n.156
  —*Crito*
    51b9–c1: 12
  —*Euthydemus*
    291c1: 39
    291c4–292b3: 40–41, 66
    291c7–8: 82
    292d6: 39
  —*Gorgias*
    454e7–8: 15
    458e: 41n.55

464b–c: 53
473e7: 9n.5
502e–503d: 35n.46
507a–c: 95n.115
507e–508a: 162n.214
515e: 12n.9
521d: 10
— *Laches*
190a–e: 37
190c8: 37n.49
190d3: 37n.49
194d9: 37n.48
— *Laws*
passim, 133–66
I 632c: 153
I 636e: 148n.188
II 657a: 143n.180
III 701d: 124n.152
III 702d–e: 138n.170
IV 704a–705b: 148
IV 714a2: 142
IV 714b: 141n.174
V 736b5–6: 138n.170
V 737c–738a: 148
V 737e7–738a2: 156–57
V 739a1–e7: 144–46
V 742d–e: 143n.180
V 744a–745a: 149
V 745b–e: 157
VI 753a: 153n.198
VI 754d–755b: 153
VI 756b–e: 152
VI 757b–c: 95n.115
VI 758a–d: 152
VI 760a–764c: 158
VI 765e: 154n.200
VI 768c–e: 154n.199
VI 769d–772d: 153
VI 772c: 154
VI 772d–785b: 150n.193

VI 779b: 148n.189
VII 820e: 101n.121
VII 793a–e: 102
X 902d–903b: 101
X 909d–910d: 151n.194
XI 919d–920c: 149n.191
XI 923a6–b2: 150n.192
XI 929e–930e: 150n.193
XII 951e5–7: 152
XII 962b4–d3: 155–56
XII 962d: 152
XII 964c: 164
XII 967b: 164
XII 966c–968a: 164n.218
— *Letters*
Letter VII, 136
— *Menexenus*
passim, 14–35
— *Meno*
92e–93c: 42
— *Phaedrus*
230b–e: 7n.10
245c–249d: 46n.61,
    116n.142
247b–248c: 64
— *Republic*
passim, 43–71
I 332c–333e: 81n.102
I 341d–342d: 73n.97
I 351a–352a: 44n.58
I 353a10–11: 54
I 353d: 44n., 59
II 368c–369a: 43–44
II 369a6–8: 138n.170
II 369b–d: 75
II 369c: 52
II 370b–c: 50
II 372d: 52
II 372e–373a: 69
II 373b–e: 69

II 374b–376c: 65n.86
III 399e: 50n., 68
III 412b–414b: 65n.86
III 412b–415e: 57
III 414b–415c: 97n.117
IV 420c2–e1: 59
IV 443a–444a: 66
IV 443c–e: 62n.83
V 449d: 49n.67
V 473d: 48n.65
VI 499b–500d: 60n.80
VI 500b8–501c3: 109–11, 115
VI 500d–501c: 68
VI 502b–d: 143n.180
VII 519c: 68n.92
VII 534b3–4: 57
VII 540c: 48n.65
VIII 557a–563d: 35n.46
IX 592b: 68, 162n.214
—*Statesman*
passim, 72–113
259c: 98
273e–275a: 83
277d–278c: 44n.58
283b–287b: 156
287d–289c: 86n.110
289c–291c: 89n.111
292a1–2: 103
293a7: 103
294a: 96
294c: 97
298d–e: 107–8
298e: 97
300b1–c6: 104–6
300c–301e: 62n.83
300c7: 105n.128
300e1–2: 106
300e11–301a3: 106
306a–e: 93

308c–311c: 130n.157
308c–309b: 92
308c1: 92
308d1: 112
308e–309b: 91
308e8: 91n.113
309b–e: 91
309b2: 91n.113
309c5–6: 94
310a–b: 91
311b–c: 91
311b8: 98
—*Timaeus*
17c–19c: 119–20
18a–c: 127
19b–c: 69n.94, 120, 132
30c–33c: 99n.118
42e–44b: 164n.218
61c–69a: 156n.201
88b6–c1: 126–27
87a–c: 127
politeia (constitution), 70, 104–6, 108, 120, 141–42
politics (political science and political technique), 5, 55, 57–58, 65–67, 72, 82, 87–88, 109n.136, 111n.137, 121–22, 129–30, 143n.181, 167
politika (political affairs), 67n.90
Proclus, 117n.143

rhetoric, 15
Rowe, Christopher J., 105n.127

Saunders, Trevor J., 134n.160, 136n.166, 156n.201, 163n.216
Smith, Adam, 61n.81

sophists, sophistry, 52, 118
soul, 45–46, 53–54, 92–93,
     115, 119, 155–56
Stalley, Richard F., 134n.159
stasis (internal strife, civil war),
     26–27
sunoikia (cohabitation), 51

Thucydides, 18–20, 28–35,
     60n.79

Vernant, Jean-Pierre, 47n.63

Vidal-Naquet, Pierre,
     157n.203–4
virtue, excellence (*aretê*),
     37–39, 51, 54–55, 80,
     92–95, 141–42, 146, 165
Vlastos, Gregory, 9n.6,
     33n.44,

women, 47–48, 145

zôon (living being, animal), 88,
     120, 126, 132